Traveling
Light

BOOKS BY ARTHUR G. McPHEE

Friendship Evangelism
Traveling Light

Traveling Light

HOW TO LIFT THE BURDENS THAT WEIGH YOU DOWN

Arthur G. McPhee

ZONDERVAN PUBLISHING HOUSE
OF THE ZONDERVAN CORPORATION
GRAND RAPIDS, MICHIGAN 49506

Scripture quotations are from the *New International Version* of the Bible (© 1978 by New York International Bible Society) unless otherwise noted. Additional translations used are:

King James Version, Zondervan Publishing House (KJV)

Revised Standard Version, © 1952 and 1971 by Division of Christian Education of the National Council of the Churches of Christ in the United States of America (RSV)

Today's English Version, Good News Bible, © 1976 by American Bible Society (TEV)

TRAVELING LIGHT: How to Lift Burdens That Weigh You Down

© 1979 by The Zondervan Corporation
Grand Rapids, Michigan

Library of Congress Cataloging in Publication Data

McPhee, Arthur, 1945-
  Traveling light. .

    1.   Christian life—Mennonite authors.   I.   Title.
BV4501.M337   248'.48'97   79-20583
Zondervan ISBN 0-310-37322-0
Choice Books: ISBN 0-310-37329-8

Printed in the United States of America

CONTENTS

Preface

TRANSFER THE LOAD

TRANSFORM THE PAST AND FUTURE

TRADE IN OLD HABITS

Preface

Many Christians wish they could be better examples of the faith they profess. They believe they have a Father in heaven who has numbered the very hairs on their heads . . . yet they worry. They say they have experienced the peace of Christ . . . yet they struggle with stress. They claim they possess transformed minds . . . yet they lust. They assert that Christ has become the very center of their lives . . . yet they are selfish. They say they have experienced Christ's liberating love . . . yet they are in bondage—to jealousy, to temper, to guilt, to depression, to any number of prisons from which they should have been freed.

Are you one of those Christians? Are there areas in which you have even less freedom than some non-Christians you know? How can that be, when, as the great apostle Paul said, "It is for freedom that Christ has set us free"? (Gal. 5:1).

Nevertheless, even the apostle Paul experienced what you have experienced. For example, in his Letter to the Romans, he lamented, "What I want to do I do not do, but what I hate I do. I have the desire to do what is good, but I cannot carry it out" (Rom. 7:15, 18). So, when Paul says, "It is for freedom that Christ has set us free," you should not take that to mean Christ doesn't understand your shortcomings or sympathize with them. On the contrary, He knows them only too well.

Unlike you and me, Paul was not intimidated or defeated by his weaknesses. He was a realist; he acknowledged the fact of sin living in him. However, he firmly maintained that God empowers His children to overcome. Led by the Spirit, the child of God has a way out of any enslavement. In the strength of Christ he can stand and withstand. "Stand firm, then," he says, "and do not let yourselves be burdened again by a yoke of slavery. You, my brothers, were called to be free" (Gal. 5:1, 13).

Thus, you and I can be free at last from every burden that weighs us down. This book will help you travel light along the road of life. In the following chapters, I will survey a number of the common problems Christians face and some Biblical principles for overcoming them.

Here is one word of warning I would add. This book is not a substitute for the more intensive help you can receive from a pastor, doctor, counselor, or caring friend. If, for example, you are suffering from acute depression, you may find the help you need in the brief discussion in this book. But the likelihood is that you will want further assistance as well. The final solution is Christ. In a very real sense, the *only* solution is Christ, but He has many ways of working: through insights that come directly from the Holy Spirit; through brotherly counsel; through the skilled hands and mind of a physician; through miraculous intervention. This book is not intended to circumvent any of those possibilities. I hope, though, that it can be used of the Lord to significantly help many: to comfort, to encourage, to strengthen, to help overcome—for the glory of God, who defeats our every foe!

—ARTHUR McPHEE

☆ ☆ ☆ ☆ ☆ ☆ ☆ ☆ ☆ ☆

TRANSFER THE LOAD

☆ ☆ ☆ ☆ ☆ ☆ ☆ ☆ ☆ ☆

*We are afraid to trust God. We want to.
We believe we can. But, somehow, we
still have a need to guide things, to be
at the controls.*

1

His Yoke Is Easy

Two Christian laymen were calling on homes in their
community in order to interest the neighbors in Christianity. At one house a stoop-shouldered man, leaning
on a cane, came to the door. "What can I do for you?"
he asked. "Well, we'd like to talk to you for a few
moments about Christianity, if you have the time," said
one of the laymen. "Christianity!" said the old man.
"Haven't I got enough problems without taking on
Christianity?"

If that man's reaction causes you to smile a bit,
perhaps it is, in part, because something about his
statement rings true. There are believers who sometimes feel that way—that Christianity is a chore, a
millstone around their neck, a dead weight on their
shoulders. At times, Christianity is just another burden
to them. The church is just another organization making
insensitive demands, when they are already overtaxed.

A pitiful incident is recorded in Isaiah about a time

when the worshipers of the pagan gods Nebo and Bel needed to hide their objects of worship in order to protect them. The enemy was approaching, so they hoisted their stone idols onto beasts of burden and attempted to transport them to safety. (The gods couldn't protect the people, you see, so the people had to protect the gods!)

The humiliating need to carry their gods off to safety wasn't the worst of it, though. The weight of the idols was so great the oxen couldn't support them, so the people had to leave their "gods" behind and fend for themselves.

But here's the rub! Is it any different for us? Is our religion less burdensome? Is the yoke of our religion any easier?

Jesus said, "Come to me, all you who are weary and burdened, and I will give you rest. Take my yoke upon you and learn from me, for I am gentle and humble in heart, and you will find rest for your souls. For my yoke is easy and my burden is light" (Matt. 11:28-30). But does that really prove to be our experience? For example, say you're a Christian businessman. It is difficult enough to earn a living these days! But when conscience fails to let you take those questionable short-cuts your competition takes, when you must continually weigh the motives and morality of even your advertising, when church agencies look to you to carry what is undoubtedly more than your fair share of the institutional burden (because, after all, aren't Christian businessmen enormously successful?), what is Christianity then? Is the yoke easy? Is the burden light?

Or say you're flat on your back in a hospital bed. What is Christianity then? When, even though you are racked with pain, you must make a stoic effort not to complain, and even to smile if you can manage it, as testimony to the grace of God which enables you not only to endure but to prevail! Or, even though you desperately need to rest and recuperate, some good brothers and sisters feel constrained to pop into your room whether it's the designated time for visitors or not. Then they make an afternoon of it while you desperately struggle to stay awake. If you're anticipating surgery, it's even worse. The visitors will plop themselves down on your bed and proceed to tell you horror stories about how Uncle Bill had the same operation and died, or about the complications that resulted when Cousin Sarah had it and the doctors left a sponge inside her.

Of course I am exaggerating, but what *is* Christianity when you're flat on your back in a hospital bed? Is the yoke easy then? Is the burden light?

Or suppose you are a laborer in a factory. What is Christianity in that setting? When your fellow workers insist upon you doing a dishonest day's work in order to keep the quotas low, when your foreman reacts to the manager's dissatisfaction by insisting that it's really you and a few others who need to shape up, or when, because of your faith, you are the object of some rather cruel fun-making and are automatically expected to turn the other cheek, what is Christianity then? Is the yoke easy? The burden light?

Or, think of the church's insistence on the responsibilities of the faithful. It refuses to allow you to take the easy way out of a marriage that's in trouble. It expects your faithful attendance at meetings. Think of the committee work, the class preparations, the struggles to improve relationships, the wrestling with issues—all of which are supposed to be vital requisites for those serious about their religion!

If it doesn't weary you to think about all those things,

consider the ridicule and persecution that often come when Christians are truly being salt. Or consider the division that sometimes comes to a family when one member becomes a Christian. "I haven't come to bring peace but a sword," said Jesus about that kind of circumstance. "A man has to give up everything, even his own life to be My disciple," He said on another occasion. "You're going to have a daily cross to bear when you follow Me."

That raises a perplexing question. What did Jesus mean by, "My yoke is easy; My burden is light"? He knew better! Time and time again He pointed out that the Christian life is not an easy road. It's a narrow road, He said; it's a sacrificial road; it's a cross-bearing road! So it *sounds* like a gross contradiction. All these poor souls taking on a yoke that's supposed to be easy and a burden that's supposed to be light. And it turns out to be just the opposite—more cumbersome, more intolerable, more oppressive, more wearisome, more unmanageable, more impossible than the old burdens! "Who does He think He's kidding?" we are tempted to ask. Talk about the inconsistencies of politicians!

And, yet, His word stands! "Come to me, all you who are weary and burdened, and I will give you rest. Take my yoke upon you and learn from me, for I am gentle and humble in heart, and you will find rest for your souls. For my yoke is easy and my burden is light."

Three imperatives in Jesus' words can help us. They are the invitations to "come," "take," and "learn."

Come

The word "come" indicates the focus of Jesus' invitation. "Come to Me," He says, "and I will give you rest." He doesn't say, "Come to a teaching." He doesn't say,

16

"Come to a philosophy." He doesn't say, "Come to an ideal or cause." He doesn't even say, "Come to a religion." He says, "Come to Me." Jesus Himself is the focus of the invitation.

That solves some of the problems right off, because much of the burden people associate with Christianity is the burden of Christianity as a religion—the structure, the institution, the formalism. But although all of those things have a role to play in the church, they are not at the heart of what we call Christianity.

For Christianity is not a religion. Christianity is not rites nor rituals. It is a relationship—a relationship with the God who chose not to remain aloof from the problems that man, through sin, acquired, but to take them upon Himself—all the way to the cross! So Christ is not the burden of religion; religion is the burden of religion! It is the externals that weigh us down!

Forms are important in Christianity in the same way bottles are important as containers: the vital thing is not the bottle; it's the drink, or the precious ointment, or whatever is in the bottle! That is what ought to concern us. When you substitute a bottle for its contents, or a flag for what it symbolizes, or religion for the intimate fellowship you can have in Christ—when you substitute external rites for the inward workings of the Spirit— then what's left is no more than the green leaf hanging on the dead branch which has been lopped off!

Take

The second imperative—the word "take"—indicates, however, that following Christ does not mean the absence of burdens. There *is* a yoke! There *is* a burden! In fact, there are lots of them. Christianity isn't escapism. Many of the cults are. They promise an end to burdens—an end to sickness and disease, an end to crises in relationships, an end to rainstorms at church picnics. They offer an escape. But for this life, Christianity offers not an escape but power—power to overcome, to prevail, to rise above any adversity, any dilemma; power to see it through! Christianity is most assuredly *not* a running away from responsibility. It is not a hiding from pain, nor death, nor anything else. No matter what anyone tries to tell you, the chores, the tasks, the crosses are still there.

But you say, "Doesn't that bring us right back to a Christianity that is just another burden?" No, there is a difference. We no longer have to bear the burden by ourselves. Christ helps us.

However, our trouble is that we are reluctant to accept His help. We are afraid to let go. We are afraid to trust the great God who is the creating and sustaining force behind the universe. We want to. We believe we can. But, somehow, we still have a need to guide things, to be at the controls.

If one member of a family does most of the driving, it is difficult for him to sleep on those infrequent occasions when someone else is at the wheel. But family members who are usually passengers do not have that problem at all. You see, they are used to exercising faith in the driver; however, the driver is used to exercising faith only in himself. In our spiritual pilgrimages, we must all be passengers. Christ is the driver; He must be at the controls while, somehow, we must learn to exercise complete faith in Him, and so to rest. We need to cast all our burdens and cares upon Him. If only we'd do that! If we would just rid ourselves of *our* yokes and try on His for size, we'd find that it fits perfectly and rides easy. We'd discover that when Christ is in the driver's seat, it really does make a difference.

Notice the personal pronouns in Jesus' statement. There *is* a yoke, but it is His yoke, not ours. There *is* a burden, but now the burden is His, and that makes it light as far as we're concerned.

A man was walking home from town with a hundred-pound sack of seed slung over his shoulder. A neighbor drove up in his pick-up and offered him a ride home. He was happy to accept. When he climbed into the cab with his bulky, heavy sack of seed, his neighbor said, "Hey, you don't need to carry that now. Just throw it in the back of the pick-up!" But the man said, "Oh, I couldn't do that. It's really kind of you to offer, but it's enough for you to carry me, let alone my sack of seed!" Don't we do that? Of course there is a sense in which Christianity means some brand-new burdens, probably many more. But they can be lighter even than the old burdens, if we'll just throw them in the back of Christ's pick-up.

Learn

The third imperative, "learn," tells us something even more significant. "Take My yoke upon you, and learn from Me," Jesus said. He didn't ask us just to take the yoke as a yoke. He asked us to come close to Him and learn His secret—the secret of bearing the yoke in His Spirit, with His objectives, with His vision and His way. It is then, and only then, that His yoke becomes easy and His burden light. It is possible to carry on *our* Christian work, rather than *His* work. When that happens, the yoke is not easy. It is also possible to carry on that work in the flesh rather than in the Spirit. When that happens, the burden is not light. But we need not find ourselves in either of those dilemmas if we will

19

learn from Him. The promise is to those who are willing to become learners and say, "I will not trust my own learning, but only what I learn at Your feet, Lord Jesus."

We all have a master, and we all wear a yoke. If it is our own yoke, we could not have a worse one. However, it might be the devil's; it might be the world's; and either of these are unbearably heavy, too. But if we take Christ as our Master, come to Him, take His yoke upon us, and learn from Him, we will find release from the burdens of life such as we never dreamed possible. No longer will we have a religion we need to bear up, but rather, a relationship that bears us up! No longer will we be forever weary in well-doing. Although we will accomplish more of significance than ever before, we will be rested—because His yoke fits—it's easy!

Christians, therefore, better than anyone, ought to know how to rest. A little boy came home from kindergarten one day and announced that the teacher had put a gold star on his report card. His mother was delighted, because the little boy was always in trouble and had never received a gold star. "Son, I'm so proud of you," she said. "What did you do to win the star?" He replied, "During rest period I rested better than anyone else."

Have you learned how to do that? Have you learned how to lay hold on the rest that's yours in Christ? Or, have you been hauling around your religion like the Babylonians hauled around Bel and Nebo?

An ancient story tells how a group of townsmen went out into the forest to gather logs for a new meetinghouse. Some of the men returned tired and exhausted. But one man was refreshed and strong, even though he returned with the heaviest burden. He had cut down a fruit tree, and as he hauled it away he occasionally paused to take nourishment from its fruit. In our struggle to build Christlike lives and conquer the burdens that come our way, we find strength as we pause to nourish our spirits at Jesus' feet. He is the One whose yoke is easy, and whose burden is light.

Thus, even though the burdens Christians bear are heavier in some respects than their former burdens, nevertheless they are lighter, because Christ is there to help. But we need to do three things:

1. We need to come to Him, to draw close.
2. We need to put our trust in Him by taking His yoke upon us.
3. We need to be willing learners, to become sensitized to His steady and sure guidance.

Come, take, learn—that's the way to rest, in Jesus.

Let there be no mistake about it, if you are truly being light, and if you are truly being salt, then your ship of faith is going to be tossed about mercilessly.

2

Weathering Spiritual Storms

There are times when we feel as if we are living in a war zone, that we are in enemy-occupied territory. Certain crises come into our lives that seem too calculated, too well-timed, too sinister to be otherwise. Just when we seem to be getting ahead in our spiritual walk, just when we are experiencing a certain degree of victory, along come these unexplained storms that seem calculated to create havoc for us.

The truth is that sometimes such storms *are* calculated. The Bible teaches that they are one of the results of the cosmic rift between God and Satan, who was once one of God's most magnificent creations. God and Satan are at war, and you and I are the battleground.

Many people, however, refuse to accept that. They snicker at such teaching. For them the devil has become a joke, a mythological caricature of evil who emerges at cocktail parties, complete with horns, tail, and pitchfork. Or else he emerges in the latest occult feature film to entertain those willing to pay for the amusement of a good scare.

People who take Satan seriously are considered strange and are often the object of snickers and sneers—we've outgrown the day when demons did their mischief, sorcerers cast their spells, and witches rode their brooms.

A cartoon had a little girl asking her playmate, "Do you believe in the devil?" to which her friend replied, "Of course not, Silly; it's like Santa Claus; it's only Daddy."

That is how we have come to think of the devil; that is how we talk about him—lightly, frivolously, the way we talk about a harmless fairy tale. But as Dr. Emile Cailliet has put it, "One of the neatest tricks Satan has ever performed is to convince so many people that he *does not* exist."

The Bible, however, takes Satan seriously. And I should think that, by merely reflecting on some of the demonic happenings in recent history, we would too. How else do you explain the horrible massacre in Jonestown, Guyana? How else do you explain a Hitler? Is there a better explanation for the power that caused nearly a thousand people to commit mass suicide, or the power that took the great and highly civilized German nation captive in the days of the Nazis?

Satan is especially interested in defeating those who have in faith received Jesus Christ as their Lord. A chilling scene in the New Testament graphically illustrates this. On the easel of our imaginations most of us have painted Jesus' meeting with His disciples in the upper room as a peaceful scene, a scene of serenity, a time of tranquillity. But if there was anything of tranquillity in that room, it was a tense tranquillity—the calm before the storm. The light that shone through the window was a fading light about to give way to black night. And the dark cloud that hung over the mountain was about to convulse that peaceful scene into a wasteland of crushed hopes and crumbled dreams. In just a brief hour or two the storm of Satan's fury would come whirling full force into the lives of all that little band and make havoc for every one of them.

Jesus knew that full well. That is why He turned to one of the disciples, saying, "Simon, Simon, Satan has asked to sift you as wheat" (Luke 22:31). That is why He asked them, "When I sent you without purse, bag or sandals, did you lack anything?" "Nothing," they answered. Then He said, "But now if you have a purse, take it, and also a bag; and if you don't have a sword, sell your cloak and buy one." The disciples misunderstood him, saying, "See, Lord, here are two swords." Even after three years with Him, they thought of Jesus' kingdom as a worldly, political kingdom—one that would come into existence by force. They did not grasp the real significance of Jesus' statement, which was a figurative one indicating that special spiritual resources would be needed to weather the spiritual storms ahead. "That is enough," said Jesus, and he dropped the subject (Luke 22:35-38).

The Bible tells us, and experience confirms it, that Satan is still wanting to sift the followers of Jesus like wheat. If you are a Christian, that means you! And, if anything, as you become a stronger Christian, and as the return of the Lord Jesus approaches, you will find the whirlwind of Satan's fury more intense than ever.

Let there be no mistake about it, if you are truly being light, and if you are truly being salt, then your ship of faith is going to be tossed about mercilessly. You will need to batten down the hatches and lay hold of every available resource to ride out the storm. You will need the resource of a steadfast faith. You will need the resource of a supportive brotherhood. And you will need the resource of a sovereign God.

A Steadfast Faith

When Jesus told Simon that Satan wanted to sift them all as wheat, He added, "But I have prayed for you, Simon, that your faith may not fail" (Luke 22:32).

Just as it takes the night to reveal the stars, so it takes times of trial to reveal the strength and steadfastness of the faith God gives us. Little did Peter realize that Satan's siege this night would be such a test for him. When Jesus told Simon Peter He had prayed for him, Peter's hasty reply was, "I am willing to go with you to prison and to death if need be." But actually his reply showed that he was utterly naive as to the real nature of the warfare ahead. His reliance upon the sword when the soldiers came to arrest Jesus confirms his lack of understanding.

Peter was thinking of outer warfare, but Satan conducts inner warfare—"war against the soul," as Peter himself later described it. Imagine Peter's shock, then, when Jesus predicted, "I tell you, Peter, before the rooster crows today, you will deny three times that you know me" (Luke 22:34). Peter lost the battle by relying on a Spartan spirit . . . but, praise God, he won the war by coming back to faith.

And that is where evil is always ultimately defeated. When the storm of Satan's fury comes into your life, the strength you will need to prevail will not come from whatever courage and grit you may have, but from the quality of faith you possess.

A Supportive Brotherhood

Not only will you need a steadfast faith to endure the storms of life, you will also need a supportive brotherhood. That is why the church is so important. In this independent age we often overlook that, but Jesus did not overlook it. Notice what He says to Simon Peter next: "Simon . . . when you turn back to me, you must strengthen your brothers" (Luke 22:32, TEV).

The anguish and shame of Peter's denials brought home to him the utter folly of reliance upon the flesh. They also brought home to him the utter reality of the power of prayer. Jesus' prayer for Peter was answered. Peter did return to his Lord, qualifying him in a very special sense to strengthen his brothers. And, likewise, who is more qualified to assist us in our ordeals than one who has been through the furnace of similar affliction?

When you are in trouble it is your duty to seek such help. Because of the spiritual nature of your warfare with Satan, it is only in the brotherhood of Christian believers that you will find that help. The world has much cheap advice to offer, but only help that is born out of experience avails. A drowning man does not grasp for floating straws, but for something more substantial. Let's be sure that is true of us as well.

A Sovereign God

To what shall we turn when the storms of life come? To a steadfast faith. To whom shall we turn in the hour of trial? To a supportive brotherhood . . . but even more importantly, to a sovereign God, through prayer. If you remember nothing else, let me encourage you to remember that! Jesus, knowing what Peter would soon be going through, remembered. He said, "Simon, I have prayed. . . ." Jesus in Gethsemane remembered. He said, "Father, if it be possible. . . ." Let us in our Gethsemanes remember it, too.

When it seems the bottom is about to drop out of the universe, when your ship is about to capsize, remember that we have a great God who is able to do exceeding abundantly more than all we ask or imagine! "Satan has asked to sift you all like wheat." Even the devil cannot act without God's permission, you see. As with Job, so with you. God is always in control, and He will not allow you to be tempted beyond what you're able to endure, but will always provide a way of escape.

When your own resources seem to be disintegrating, His are available—His faith, His church, even He Himself. The things that fall apart in Satan's storms are man-made, nothing more.

The earth does not tip over on its axis. The mountains do not collapse. The seasons still follow right on schedule. The sun and the moon and the stars stay on their courses. We still have a world, and God is still in control! His eternal purposes are going to win out, and, laying hold of the resources of a steadfast faith, a supportive brotherhood, and a sovereign God, you will win out, too. You will not merely endure the storms of life, but you will ultimately prevail!

Most people regard trouble as something to avoid. Another way to view trouble: as opportunity—as something which, despite its unpleasantness, can produce good.

3

Turning Adversity Into Opportunity

I would have preferred to visit Jim in his hospital room, but since I had a cold, I decided to phone him instead. I was feeling a bit under the weather, but I knew that Jim, who had been in a serious accident, must be feeling much worse.

"Hi, Jim, how are you?" I asked.

"I'm great! But listen, the doctor just came into the room. Can you call me back in a few minutes?"

"Sure," I said.

I placed the receiver on the cradle and shook my head. Feeling great? I thought. After having been nearly killed? And that was not all. The accident was just one of a series of ordeals this young man had been through recently. This was his third brush with death in a year! It sounded strange to hear someone who'd been through all he had say that he felt great.

I have known others who could face trouble that way. Take Scott, a teen-ager who had fallen from the face of a cliff, a thousand miles from home. Knowing absolutely no one in our community, he was forced to remain in traction in the local hospital for weeks. Yet, not once did I hear him complain. Nor did I ever find him in an uncheerful mood.

Or take Jill, a vibrant, vivacious young woman with everything to live for; yet she learned one day that she had only months to live. However, the knowledge of her impending death did not diminish her cheery appearance or her radiant character in the slightest. If anything, she seemed even more cheerful.

It is wrong, though, to imagine that such persons escape dealing with anxiety and depression altogether. Studdard Kennedy used to say that the man or woman who does not find suffering and pain a distressful thing has either hardening of the heart or softening of the brain. Feelings of distress always come with trouble. Though we may camouflage them, they are normal. Stoicism is not a normal trait of human nature.

So, Jim, Scott, and Jill were not remarkable because they escaped trauma—be assured, they did not escape it. Rather, it was the inner resources of strength they laid hold of that gave them the ability to rise above their circumstances. The other day I greeted a friend with a "How are you today?" to which he responded, "Pretty well, under the circumstances." So I said to him, "What are you doing under there?" But these young people were not "under the circumstances," they were on top. There was no need whatever to ask *them* such a question.

You, too, can face trouble and not be defeated by it. I believe this because I have seen many friends whose faces were aglow, even though they had good reason to be in the depths of despair. Inner resources of strength

29

are available to all of us, through which we, like Jim, Scott, and Jill, can be overcomers, too.

A New Perspective

There are several crucial differences between the man or woman who overcomes trouble and the one who is overcome by trouble. One difference is that the overcomer has a unique perspective on trouble.

Most people regard trouble as something to be avoided at all costs. If they cannot avoid it, they become bitter and despairing, or they try to deny their trouble by drowning it in drink or fantasies or some other "pain killer." Another way to view trouble is as an opportunity—as something which, despite its unpleasantness, can produce good.

Have you ever had the experience of being swept off your feet and thrown down by one of those monstrous walls of water that plow into certain of the world's beaches? Experience has taught me to high-tail it when I see one coming, although I still see them too late sometimes. But a surfer does just the opposite. He paddles his board right out to one of the giants, watching it carefully as it develops. Then, just when the wave reaches up its watery paw as if to pound him to the bottom, he gets to his feet and rides it into shore! It is a breathless experience, even for the spectator! Instead of being buried by the wave, the surfer uses it to his advantage. He turns his experience from something ominous into something beautiful.

Every kind of trouble has that potential for good. The old Puritans used to say about illness, for example, that the worst kind of affliction is a "dumb" one—that is, one that doesn't teach you anything. Maltbie Babcock reflected that, "The tests of life are to make, not break us. Trouble may demolish a man's business but build up his character. The blow at the outer man may be the greatest blessing to the inner man. If God, then, puts or permits anything hard in our lives, be sure that the real peril, the real trouble, is that we shall lose if we flinch or rebel."[1] I am convinced that if everyone had such insight into the beneficial side of trouble, there would be far fewer defeated persons in the world. A short-sighted perspective on trouble defeats more persons than trouble itself. We need to realize, as someone humorously put it, "There may be a last straw that breaks the camel's back, but a large proportion of the other straws serve to develop its muscles." Isn't it sad that so many broken human beings have *not* realized that?

The apostle Paul knew something of the built-in opportunities of trouble. Here, for instance, is what he wrote to the church at Corinth:

> Praise be to the God and Father of our Lord Jesus Christ, the Father of compassion and the God of all comfort, who comforts us in all our troubles, so that we can comfort those in any trouble with the comfort we ourselves have received from God. For just as the sufferings of Christ flow over into our lives, so also through Christ our comfort overflows. If we are distressed, it is for your comfort and salvation; if we are comforted, it is for your comfort, which produces in you patient endurance of the same sufferings we suffer. And our hope for you is firm, because we know that just as you share in our sufferings, so also you share in our comfort (2 Cor. 1:3-7).

Paul had come through an ordeal in which he had personally experienced God's mercy and comfort. He was not only strengthened and encouraged, but was shown that just as Jesus' suffering on the cross resulted in benefit to others, so his own suffering could benefit the Corinthians. For one thing, his trouble had better equipped him to endure even more difficult trials in his service to them. For another thing, the Corinthians, in their own troubles, would know that just as God had strengthened Paul, so He would strengthen them.

So, Paul had a different perspective on trouble than many of us. To be sure, he regarded it as an ordeal, as very unpleasant business, but he also saw that it had another side, a built-in potential for good.

An additional perspective on trouble helps us face it with courage. It is simply this: trouble comes to an end. As one of the Psalms says, "Trouble endures but for the night; joy comes in the morning."

I once heard about an old man who always wore a smile on his face and a twinkle in his eye. Someone asked him how he could always be so cheerful.

His answer was, "I get it out of the Bible."

"You get it out of the Bible?" came the reply.

"Yup. Over and over in the Bible I see the words, 'And it came to pass,' but never does it say, 'And it came to stay.'"

Now, we may have trouble with the man's exegesis, but we cannot find fault with the truth he stated. Trouble is a temporary phenomenon that gives us grief for the moment, but in the end it strengthens us and equips us with renewed stamina for the trials of kingdom work.

That is why James could say of trouble:

Consider it pure joy, my brothers, whenever

you face trials of many kinds, because you know that the testing of your faith develops perseverance. Perseverance must finish its work so that you may be mature and complete, not lacking anything (James 1:2-4).

Like Paul, James had laid hold of the inner strength of a God-given insight into trouble's other side.

Troubles Are for Sharing

So the first difference between those who are trouble's victims and those who have victory over trouble is their unique perspective on it. A second difference is the God-given realization that troubles are not something you keep to yourself.

There is a sense in which that seems obvious. If you are struggling with something and you want encouragement and help, you don't bury your problem and tell no one about it. You share it. You can do so with a friend, in a small group, in a minister's study, or in a psychologist's or physician's office. You can say to your friend or small group, for example, "You know, I just can't seem to get along with so-and-so." You can say to your minister, "I've been having serious lapses in my moral conduct recently that I know I need to put right." You can say to your physician, "I'm having severe abdominal pain, and I need to know what I should do."

But there is another way to share your trouble, which is not so obvious. Instead of sharing the burden, you share the comfort you have received.

Let me give you an example. Have you ever received financial help from a friend when you were in a bind? Sooner or later that is a comforting reprieve you'll be able to give someone else when financial trouble overtakes him. Have you ever gone through a period of intense doubt about your faith? Well, the help you received in your trouble is likely to be of significant help to others you know when, suddenly, doubts come to haunt them.

One of the women in our church told me recently how her bouts with depression and her victory over them were now proving to be just the background she needed to help a neighbor who was also wrestling with depression. I am sure that is what the apostle Paul had in mind when he wrote about the comfort he had received, *overflowing* to help others: "If we are distressed, it is for your comfort and salvation; if we are comforted, it is for your comfort, which produces in you patient endurance of the same sufferings we suffer" (2 Cor. 1:6). I like the way it is put in the Book of Proverbs, too: "Friends always show their love. What are brothers for if not to share trouble?" (17:17, TEV).

Raymond Linquist said that life's greatest waste is not the waste that results from a forest fire or the wasted tons of water that plummet unused over countless waterfalls. He said it is not even the wasted billions that keep us up to our necks in the arms race. Rather, it is "the enormous amount of personal suffering that never gets invested."

There are many ways in which we can invest trouble: in the establishment of inner fortitude to cope; in the stretching of our minds to realize that more significant things are in the world than the physical comfort of the body; and, as we have seen, in the gift of comfort to those who are facing troubles of the same kind we have faced.

Just that realization—that our trouble can be invested for good, especially for the good of others—is a kind of strength in itself. That, along with the more basic understanding that trouble always contains a built-in potential for good, is just the strength we need to cope.

He Is Able

But the real measure of that inner strength is the measure of Christ in our lives. It is the final realization that He is able: able to see us through any troubles that come; able to provide a way of escape; able not only to help us endure, but prevail. As Paul discovered, His grace is sufficient.

I can tell you the truth about trouble: by facing it with the right frame of mind, you can turn it into triumph. I can point out that the experience of trouble lays the foundation for helping others through similar struggles later on. But until Jesus makes the truth of those facts dawn on you, and you become convinced that He is able to change your attitude toward trouble and help you employ it for good, trouble will still be trouble for you. However, once you come to understand that there really is more than eternal optimism in these insights you will no longer be defeated when difficulties come along. When you realize that the living Christ, who overcame the greatest trouble of all, is able to help you employ troubles practically, all your troubles will be turned into triumphs through Him.

Let me summarize. We can lay hold of powerful inner resources for turning trouble into triumph if we realize three things: (1) that all trouble has built-in potential for good; (2) that our troubles cannot only be good for us, but good for others; and (3) that Jesus Christ is able to assist us in employing our troubles for good.

---

[1]Quoted by Gerald Kennedy in *A Second Reader's Notebook* (New York: Harper and Brothers, 1959), p. 330.

☆ ☆ ☆ ☆ ☆ ☆ ☆ ☆ ☆ ☆ ☆ ☆

TRANSFORM
THE PAST AND FUTURE

☆ ☆ ☆ ☆ ☆ ☆ ☆ ☆ ☆ ☆ ☆ ☆

What do you do when the ghosts of yes-
eryear come back to disturb the pres-
ent? How do you cope with the grief,
with the broken relationships, with the
guilt, with the tragedies, with the
missed opportunities of the past? How
do you keep those unpleasant memories
from overwhelming the now?

4

The Ghosts of Yesteryear

Charles Dickens' "The Haunted Man" is a chilling tale
about a chemist who is plagued by thoughts of his past.
Sitting before his fire in gloomy reverie, suddenly he is
confronted by a phantom who offers him a gift of forget-
fulness. An accord is reached and not only is the man
left without a memory, but he is given the power to erase
other men's memories as well. But the result is worse
misery than before, so the story ends with a plea for the
phantom to restore his every recollection, both good and
bad, and with the man's fervent prayer, "Lord, keep my
memory green."

Most of us are haunted by unpleasant memories too,
which we, like the chemist, would gladly jettison if the
opportunity came.

Take Jan, for example. Jan's marriage had been a
wonderful, glorious experience. A great husband. Two

wonderful children. The marriage she'd always dreamed of. But one hot summer day her husband died.

Jan had many fond memories, but the memory of that day always seemed to overshadow them. She experienced a physical emptiness that never left her. The knot in her chest was dissolved only through hard sobbing. As she later put it, "I knew that only by stopping the past from overwhelming the present could I have any hope for the future."

Hal's past came to haunt him in a different way. He would wake up in the middle of the night, painfully remembering his childhood fear of being caught by his family in some of his early sexual fantasies and escapades. Or he would remember the friend who had written him just the helpful note of encouragement he had needed when he was down, a note he had intended to answer but somehow never got around to. And now the friend had died.

Addie's past contained a horrible incident in which a friend was accidentally killed at his hand. Shot to death. And though his whole life from there on out seemed to some to be a Herculean effort to atone for the mistake, and though he later became a much-respected candidate for the presidency of the United States, it seems certain that he was haunted to the end by the visitations of that childhood tragedy.

So what do you do when the ghosts of yesteryear come back to disturb the present? How do you cope with the grief, with the broken relationships, with the guilt, with the tragedies, with the missed opportunities of the past? How do you keep those unpleasant memories from overwhelming the now? How do you subdue once and for all those ghostly intruders from another day, a day you would rather forget?

For one thing, it's important to remember the good things we'd be missing in memory's absence. Most memories are pleasant reminders, windows on our past we would not wish to be without. They are a return to forgotten delights, stored away in the attic of the mind: old, familiar faces; favorite toys; kitchen smells; special achievements; special friendships.

But memory is more than an old scrapbook we like to visit; it is also a teacher. It teaches us that even the minor happenings in our lives have enduring consequences. Our lives are the sum of all we've met along the way.

I was struck by that just the other day when I happened to meet a dog, named Amos. He marched straight through a muddy pool and gave me a hug, warm as you please, though we were strangers. In the process he left his signature on my chest in indelible puddle. Later, when I got to thinking about it, I realized how many others had also left their signatures upon my life—more than I could count. I thought of some who influenced me over a long period of time, and others whose paths and mine intersected only for a moment but whose impact had been just as great. What had that to say with respect to my responsibility to those I influence along the way? I'd learned an important lesson.

So memory has a positive side too, one that I should not wish to be without. Do you remember the legend from Greek mythology, which had a woman coming down to the River Styx for ferrying over to the region of departed spirits? Charon, the ferryman, reminded the woman that if she wished, she could drink the waters of Lethe and forget the life she was leaving. This appealed to her, because, as she put it: "This means that I will forget how I have suffered." "And how you have rejoiced," said Charon. The woman continued, "I will forget my failures." "Yes," said Charon, "and your successes." "I will also forget how I have been hated," she said. "True," said the old ferryman, "but also how you have been loved." The woman thought the matter over for a moment and decided to reverse her decision to drink the Lethe potion. She would retain her memory of the bad, in order never to forget the good.

False Guilt

But there are also the scars—there is no use denying it. It is true that memory brings back pleasant things, but it also brings back ugly things, about which we feel guilty. Sometimes, however, we feel guilty when it seems we should not. Is there such a thing as false guilt?

Julie came to her pastor in tears one day, saying that she'd been miserable for months—ever since the death of her husband. (He had died of a heart attack.) In the midst of Julie's grieving it occurred to her that her husband had been acting strangely during his last few months. He seemed tired, short of breath, and he had been eating less than usual. Julie began to feel guilty. The symptoms were obvious, she thought to herself. Why wasn't I more attentive? It all could have been prevented if I'd only paid more attention. Over and over Julie rehearsed what she felt was negligence on her part that had resulted in her husband's death.

Julie's pastor said that such thoughts are common after the death of a loved one. But, although such thoughts may not be avoidable, the guilt they suggest is false guilt.

"But how can you say that?" Julie protested. "How can you say that some guilt is real and some is false? How is it possible to feel guilty if you're not?"

"Answer me this," said Julie's pastor. "Did you neglect your husband during those last few months?" (He knew that she had not.) "Actually, didn't you spend an extended amount of time with him on that cross-country vacation you'd always dreamed about? And, if I recall correctly, didn't the two of you team teach one of our Sunday school classes last quarter?"

"Yes, that's true. But that doesn't excuse my not being alert to those signs, Pastor!"

"And, Julie, do you recall any way in which you willfully closed your ears to anything God may have been telling you during that time about your husband's health? That's really the key, Julie. It's got to do with intent."

"For me, it's not that simple," Julie replied. "If I can remember those things now, I must have at least had some awareness of them then. Somehow, I can't avoid the feeling that if I'd been more sensitive, I'd have known God *was* trying to make me aware of my husband's symptoms."

"So, you're saying that you can't buy the idea of false guilt."

"Well, to an extent I can. But I can point to specific things I was aware of but not attentive to. Of course, I didn't willfully decide to take risks; but it would have been in my power to do *something* had I only been more sensitive."

"Well, perhaps the two things cannot be divided as neatly as I thought," said the pastor. "But of this I'm sure, Julie, it is wrong to keep on rehearsing these things as you have. You have a loving heavenly Father who is anxious to forgive you of any shortcomings, willful or not. In fact, He gave His Son to make it possible."

The Power of Confession

I've told Julie's story for this reason. Perhaps God has a good purpose even for what some persons have considered false guilt. Perhaps, as in Julie's case, He wants to create greater sensitivity by reminding us of insensitivity in the past. But, whether or not guilt feelings are warranted, there is no need to nurse such unpleasant memories. Our consciences can be cleansed of guilt by a simple act of confession. Thus, even bad memories can produce good. Ultimately the only harmful thing is the inappropriate way in which we handle them.

Other Scars

Some of the unpleasant memories we have, however, do not have anything to do with guilt. In fact, they often concern the wrongs someone else does to us.

The recurrence of this type of bad memory usually indicates that we're harboring hostility. Somehow it is even easier to hold others accountable than ourselves. The roots of such bitterness are legion, the consequences damning, the way out difficult.

Persuaded by her boyfriend's false affection, Peggy set aside her standards one night. When she learned she'd become pregnant, she told her friend and he promptly deserted her. Bitterness ensued. It's now been five years, and still Peggy hasn't been able to forgive. What is even more alarming, though, is the fact that she has become bitter toward all men.

Philip, betrayed by his wife, is also consumed with

bitterness. The pain of a divorce, the emotional toll paid by the children, and his wife's rejection all add up to a pill he cannot swallow. He trusted her completely. Now he asks himself how he can ever trust anybody again. A paralysis of mind and spirit has set in that's turned his emotions and powers of reasoning into concrete. Some of Philip's friends believe his bitterness runs so deep now that he may never find his way out.

Paul is in a similar fix. He's had six jobs in five years. He has experienced rejection again and again. Right or wrong he feels the fault is with others. As a result, he's allowed resentment to infect all of his relationships and he is practically friendless. So are his children, because he has infected them with his negativism and refusal to forgive.

I could point to many more examples, but what I am getting at is this. Unpleasant memories of how others have treated us can provide valuable lessons on how we should *not* treat the persons to whom we are presently relating. But, again, we needn't nurse these memories. Instead, we can disburse them by practicing forgiveness—the same forgiveness we have received many times over in Christ. Forgiveness itself is a tremendously freeing thing, but refusing to forgive is bondage.

If only we could have the attitude of Robert E. Lee, when bitter memories eat away at us. When the Civil War was over Robert E. Lee decided to accept the presidency of a little college in Virginia. Some diehards who wanted to continue the war came to him and proposed a campaign of guerilla warfare. They refused to let go of their bitterness. But Lee said, "No. The war is over. Raise your sons to be Americans." Then he devoted his final years to teaching a few young men to be good citizens and good leaders. Lee believed deeply in the cause for which he fought, but when the cause was lost, he refused to become a bitter man.

I remember reading a story about Leonardo da Vinci. According to the story, while da Vinci was busy painting *The Last Supper*, he had a bitter quarrel with one of his friends. They parted avowed enemies. Da Vinci was so aroused that when he painted Judas Iscariot, he gave him the face of his former friend. But from that moment on he had no peace. So ill at ease was he that the work came almost to a standstill. In particular, when he tried repeatedly to paint the face of Jesus, he could not do it. The vision was lost. Finally, however, Leonardo realized what his bitterness was doing to him. He went to his friend and asked for forgiveness. When the two men had forgiven each other, the vision of the face of Christ came back to him immediately, and he was able to complete the painting.

When Jesus taught the disciples what we now call the Lord's Prayer, he added a bit of commentary on one of the petitions—the petition that asks: "Forgive us our debts, as we also have forgiven our debtors" (Matt. 6:12). "For if you forgive men when they sin against you," He said, "your heavenly Father will also forgive you. But if you do not forgive men their sins, your Father will not forgive your sins" (Matt. 6:14-15).

His point was that forgiving and being forgiven go together. They can't be separated. If we refuse to forgive, we cut ourselves off from the forgiveness of others. If we forgive, not only does God forgive us, but bitterness is driven out of our hearts for good. The unpleasant memories are washed away and replaced with a freed spirit—free to love, free to praise, free to remember the best of the past instead of the worst.

Guilt cannot be repressed, excused, or coped with. It is too explosive for the first, too real for the second, and too big for the third.

5

And Now a Word From Your Conscience

You see him out of the corner of your eye, but it's too late. A state policeman has already clocked you on his radar and will at any moment be in pursuit. There's no way I can deny it, you say to yourself. I'm caught and I'm guilty. But, maybe, if I'm extra courteous he'll only give me a warning. Fat chance! Here he comes now, and he doesn't look especially friendly!

Conscience

Nobody wants to get caught by radar on the highway. But there's a kind of built-in radar in each of us that catches us often. One little girl described it as a many-pointed star that is always pricking you. Adults merely call it *conscience*. When we do something we know is wrong, conscience does prick us, although perhaps the better word would be "stab."

The Bible has some things to say about conscience. In his First Epistle, Peter mentions it twice: first, as a "conscience toward God" (2:19, KJV); and second, he speaks of "having a good conscience" (3:16, KJV). It is interesting to me how many of the great men of history have also had something to say about it. Lord Byron described it this way: "Nor ear can hear nor tongue can tell the tortures of that inward hell!" Fielding called it, "The only incorruptible thing about us." Luther said, "I am more afraid of my own heart than of the pope and all his cardinals. I have within me the great pope, self."

What is conscience? What is its value? What part does it play in life? How much heed ought we to pay it? Do we listen to it when it pronounces us guilty? Just how seriously do we take it?

Well, first of all, let's notice some of the general things regarding conscience that are found in the New Testament. What are some of the things the New Testament says conscience does? Well, we're told it bears witness, it gives testimony, and it produces action. There are certain things, for example, we say we do "for conscience's sake." How is the conscience described? As "good," as "void of offense," as "pure," and as "toward God." But that is only half the picture. It is also described as "weak," as "seared with a hot iron," as "defiled," and "evil." Doesn't help much, does it? It sounds contradictory. These descriptions do not really give us much of a picture of conscience at all.

There is no clear-cut definition of conscience in the Bible, but there is one passage of Scripture that seems to come quite close to a definition. It is Proverbs 20:27: "The lamp of the Lord searches the spirit of a man; it searches out his inmost being." In other words, in each of us there is a light that shines and searches us; through that light God speaks to us about right and wrong.

48

Conscience Must Be Educated

To take it a step further, I would say that the word you get from your conscience depends upon its understanding of right and wrong. Normally, it is a warning against the bad and an urging toward the good. It reveals goodness as goodness and badness as badness. It calls things by their right name. It calls a spade a spade, a lie a lie, and deceit deceit. It probably won't prevent you from doing those things, but it will make you feel troubled about them. However, what you get out of your conscience depends upon what you put into it, as we shall see.

Where does conscience come from? It comes from God. Remember?—it is a lamp that God holds up to our spirit, with which He searches us. Does that mean conscience is always right? No. For example, if we educate our conscience with some standard other than God's, it will misinform us. Or, if we do not listen to it, something else happens. It becomes weakened. It will not react with the readiness it once did. It will become seared, as if branded with a hot iron. It will become more and more contaminated until it is useless. It will turn to Teflon, rationalizing every action, letting every wrong deed slip by, never making us feel guilty or accountable. So it's like a computer—what we get out of it depends upon what we feed into it. And it is like any machine—if we abuse it, it will eventually break down.

But if we educate or re-educate our consciences with the knowledge of God's Word and way and will, then it can be one of the greatest gifts in our possession. All of us have a bent toward sinning. Ever since the fall of Adam and Eve, the human race has had to struggle with a depraved nature. A rightly educated conscience is like a compass; it helps to keep us on course. When we do wrong, it acts as a sentinel and warns us. It makes us feel guilty.

Dealing With Guilt

Guilt, however, must be dealt with. It is damaging to the mind and body to carry around guilt feelings and not deal with them. Unresolved guilt is harmful. When we continually feel guilty, we are robbed of peace and happiness, of confidence, of a good relationship with God.

Often we deal with guilt by less than satisfactory methods. Sometimes we attempt to repress it, but when we do we become like a steaming teakettle that's been sealed tight; eventually we are going to explode. Other times we try to rationalize our guilt. We call sin by some other name: we call it a slip, an innocent mistake; we call it sickness; we call it our background; we call it the influence of friends who weren't really friends; we call it a bad habit. We rationalize our guilt feelings a thousand ways. There is a third unsatisfactory method of reacting to our consciences. We respond by trying to remake ourselves. That, for example, is the purpose of our New Year's resolutions. But in the end, this, like the other approaches, is not the answer.

Guilt cannot be repressed, excused, or coped with. It is too explosive in its effect for the first, too real for the second, and too big for the third. But we don't need to repress guilt; we don't need to rationalize it; we don't need to cope with it; because God has already taken care of it. All we need to do is admit our sin and ask for God's forgiveness. Actually, he has already forgiven us through the cross; all we need to do is embrace His forgiveness. Until He does, all the things we're going to be talking about in the next section of this book can be overwhelming burdens—anger, jealousy, gluttony, laziness, lust, pride, alcoholism, avarice, and all the rest of the sins we commonly struggle with. The more we try to get them off our backs the more frustrated we become. Instead of feeling cleaner, we feel dirtier.

A traveler in Italy stayed overnight at a small out-of-the-way inn. The floor in his room was dreadfully dirty. He thought to himself, I'll get the maid to scrub it. Then he looked more carefully and discovered the floor was made of mud. The maid could scrub for a year, and the more she scrubbed, the worse it would get.

But God does cleanse us of guilt, and He lifts the burden of it. As John puts it, when our hearts condemn us there is Someone greater than our hearts. We can turn to the One who lifts every burden and makes our travel truly light.

The life of a man is a diary in which he means to write one story and writes another, and his humblest hour is when he compares the volume as it is with what he vowed to make it.

—James Barrie.

6

Living Out Your Ideals

Have you ever considered the role of attitude in accomplishing your goals in life? "How I Won Wimbledon," an article by Virginia Wade, got me to thinking about it. When I spotted the article, I asked myself, "How *did* this perennial loser finally manage to realize her ideal of becoming the world's best woman tennis player?" After sixteen years of defeats, she had somehow found the key to victory. What was it? "Attitude," said Virginia. She was sure the many defeats had been at least partly the result of defeatism.

That is true for many of the rest of us, too. I am a supreme realist and have always believed we need to be honest about our limitations. But I have begun to see that it is also true that most of us fall far short of what we could be, and even of our own too-timid ideals. In other words, we are defeated by our fear of defeat. We do not dare to dream God's best for us, and even the dreams we do dream, we allow to fade. After awhile we think it's safe to lower our sights, and we do. It's safe, perhaps—but it's also tragic! As Virginia Wade put it, "There's a fundamental safety in being able to say, 'That's the way it's always been,' or, 'That's the way I am'—with the implication that that's the way it's going to stay. It takes tremendous effort and singlemindedness to effect a change in something so profound as your basic self."

It's a rare person who has not experienced a few setbacks as the result of trying to play it safe. Our fear of defeat has left most of us with vanished dreams and unkept resolutions. Do you remember the times when you enrolled in school or began a new job with your battery charged and your gas tank full? You had great expectations. They were probably short-lived, however, and far sooner than you would have believed, you found the charge wearing down and the gas running out. I think, if we're honest, that's happened at times to most of us. We have often failed to live up to our ideals, haven't we?

In one of his tales, James Barrie put it this way:

> The life of a man is a diary in which he means to write one story and writes another, and his humblest hour is when he compares the volume as it is with what he vowed to make it.

There was a time when my life was headed along that course. I was aiming at a score of things, but I was hitting nothing. My aspirations were high, but my attainments were pitiable. The clear vision of my high ideals was becoming blurred, because time after time I was settling for mediocrity.

Now, if you have experienced any of that, I think you

will agree with me that when you finally see what's happening, it's frightening. I kept thinking about one of T. S. Eliot's characters. Over and over his lament would come back to haunt me. He said, "I have measured out my life with coffee spoons." I kept thinking of looking back over a life distinguished only by its non-achievements. I felt defeated.

But, then, one day I began to reflect seriously on the lives of some of the men of action in the Book of Acts in the Bible . . . on the lives of men like Peter, and James, and John, and Philip, and Stephen, and, of course, the great apostle Paul, and I began to realize that what James Barrie said isn't necessarily so! Our ideals do not need to give way to mediocrity! For here were men who lived out their ideals!

Take Paul. Once he said, "I don't count my life worth anything. I just want to finish running my race and doing the work the Lord Jesus entrusted to me, declaring the good news of God's love" (Phil. 3:8, *paraphrased*).

Well, did he? Did Paul manage to live out those ideals? Did he *finish* doing the work Jesus had entrusted him with? I think there can be no question but that he did!

Follow Paul from that point on and see if he did not! Follow him to Jerusalem and hear him declare the good news of God's love to King Agrippa. Follow him to Malta and see him doing the work of Jesus by healing the sick. Follow him to Rome and watch him expounding the Word from morning till evening. Follow him to Spain, where he undoubtedly did the same, and back to Rome again where he wrote, "I have fought the good fight, I have finished the race" (2 Tim. 4:7).

But how did he do it? Many of us know what it is to

start with a bang and end with a whimper. But what does it take to start with a bang and end with a bang as Paul did, and Stephen, and James, and Peter, and so many other great men of the Book of Acts and of the Bible as a whole? What does it take to face death as they did? What does it take to return love for hatred? What does it take to give good for evil? To put aside all selfishness? To live wholly for others? To be able to say, as Paul said, "I don't count *my* life worth anything"?

What is the source of that kind of staying power? What are the resources, the secrets—call them what you will—that enable you to follow through on your ideals and live them out to the end?

That's a crucial question, isn't it? Because no matter how great the beginning, it means nothing without a great ending. The best foundation is worthless without a superstructure. The best down payment is worthless without the last payment.

If Jesus had quit at Gethsemane, if He had said, "Lord, My will, not Thine," if He had not been able to say, "It is finished," what would we think of Him today? Would we honor Him as we do? Would we serve Him, as the Son of God? Would we call Him Lord?

Let me suggest, very quickly, three important factors in the kind of staying power that Christ had, that Paul and the apostles had, and so many great Christians since.

You Need an Objective

Paul had an objective. He knew where he was going. He was out to finish his race, to do the work the Lord Jesus had entrusted to him, "to declare the good news of God's love."

There is a difference between having ideals and

having an objective. Ideals are general; an objective is specific. I'm talking about a cause, something bigger than you are that you can give yourself to, so you can say with Paul, "I don't count my *life* worth anything . . . I've got an objective, and that's what's important: doing the work the Lord Jesus entrusted to me, declaring the good news of God's love!" So you need an objective.

You Need Accountability

The success of any runner is determined in part by accountability: accountability to the coach, to the team, to the fans. And so it is with our lives. Without accountability, we are just not going to be able to live out those ideals of ours. Without accountability, we are going to settle for mediocrity every time. Without accountability we may get off to a good start, but we will never finish the race with the kind of record we had hoped for.

Paul had accountability . . . "I just want to finish . . . doing the work the Lord Jesus entrusted to me." You see, declaring the good news of God's love was more than an objective for Paul—it was a trust!

You Need an Enabler

Paul never lost sight of the fact that although Jesus had entrusted him with a specific work, the work, nevertheless, remained Jesus' work! Paul never lost sight of the fact that for the work to succeed, Jesus had to be in charge!

Thus, not only will you find an objective in the cause of Christ, not only will you find accountability in Him, but you will also find One who will share the burden of that accountability with you! For not only does Jesus give us the desire to live out our ideals, not only does He give us the conscience, but He also gives us the strength!

When Jesus trusts us to do a job, He, nevertheless, remains in charge. But because He remains in charge, He shares the objective and the burden of the accountability with us. Through the Holy Spirit He equips us, motivates us, strengthens us, and sustains us! Our part is simply to trust Him completely. We are to rely on His provisions to run the race, not on our own strength.

The author of Hebrews puts it well. He pictures us running this race of life with a great crowd of the saints of old in the stands as spectators. Here is what he says to us:

> Therefore, let us lay aside all our encumbrances, and the sin that so easily trips us up, and let us run with endurance the race that is before us, keeping our eyes on Jesus (Heb. 12:1-2, *from the Greek*).

That's it, you see! Looking to Jesus! Keeping our eyes fixed on Jesus! Jesus as our objective. Jesus, to whom we must give account. Jesus, who alone makes it possible for us to finish the race and live out our ideals triumphantly!

There is a fruitfulness that flourishes even though the body is declining, a fruitfulness which makes old age something to look forward to after all, which makes the autumn of life a welcome friend, too.

7

Is There Life After Retirement?

The morns are meeker than they were
The nuts are getting brown
The berry's cheek is plumper
The Rose is out of town.[1]

What is it about frosty old Autumn that makes the blood run hot with excitement? Is it the brilliant, festive costumes the hardwoods wear? Is it the prospect of a new school year with a fresh start? Or is it the cool reprieve that comes with sultry summer's dissipation? Whatever it is, for must of us, the autumn of the year is a welcome friend.

But not so, the autumn of life. The autumn of life is an intruder, a thief, a pillager who is to be avoided at all costs. The only trouble is that Old Age can't be avoided. He can't be run from, or tricked, or denied. There is no Fountain of Youth for any price! Half a thousand years ago, Ponce de Leon searched for it in vain, and it cost him his life.

A thousand years ago an unknown Japanese poet wished:

> If only, when one heard
> That Old Age was coming
> One could bolt the door,
> Answer, 'Not at home'
> And refuse to meet him![2]

But, for all his wishing, the poet could not have refused to meet life's autumn, and neither shall we.

Old Age goes out of his way to meet us all. And unless death takes us early, he will not be put off. So, even though old age may seem a long way off to you right now . . . even though, despite short days, the years seem long . . . it will not be long at all until the days will be long, but the years short, and Old Age will have at last embraced you.

Thus, it seems to me, that whether you are young or old, the appropriate question concerning the autumn of life is not one of avoidance or denial, but of attitude.

In his novel, *Coningsby*, Benjamin Disraeli wrote: "Youth is a blunder; manhood a struggle; Old Age a regret." And that is very likely true for the man who does not know God.

The Promise of Fruitfulness

But for the righteous person, old age need not be a regret at all. Just the opposite, in fact. For the Bible promises that righteous people shall "still bring forth fruit in old age, they are ever full of sap and green" (Ps. 92:14 RSV). Even though the decaying, degenerating influence of old age may be making its mark on the body, even though, in a sense, the bloom of peak years may have faded, even though it is accurate to say with

59

Emily Dickinson that "the Rose is out of town," it is also true to say that, in the Christian, old age reveals a maturity, a ripening, a fullness that was not evident before. They shall "still bring forth fruit in old age, they are ever full of sap and green."

The man the psalmist speaks of is like the olive tree, which bears fruit even when it is very old and its trunk is nothing more than a shell. But is it really true? Can you and I really expect that kind of an old age? Will the autumn of our lives be as fruitful as the psalmist says it will? Or is he mouthing empty rhetoric?

If what he says is really true, then old age would be much easier to face, because the prospect of being useless is our greatest worry about living into our seventies and eighties—that and death. But if it's really true that we can expect to go on bearing fruit, if it's really true that we can expect to flourish; then, that will go a long way toward giving us a more positive and optimistic attitude about our latter years.

Well, for a lot of people it has been true! Think of E. Stanley Jones, for example, whose ministry was as powerful and productive in his seventies as it was when he was a young man. Or think of Grandma Moses and the art she produced during a time of life when most people are all washed up. Or think of Michelangelo, still busy at his inspired work through his eighties. Or Titian, who finished his masterpiece, *The Last Supper*, at eighty. Or Goethe, who finished *Faust*, his finest achievement, at age eighty-one.

The Characteristics of the Fruit

But I think what the psalmist had in mind goes beyond that. He is not thinking of productivity in just that sense. He is thinking of another kind of fruitfulness, a richer kind, with a yield that is more lasting. He is thinking of what the New Testament writers came to call "the fruit of the Spirit." He is thinking of a fruitfulness that comes only to the person who is right with God.

How does this fruit manifest itself in old age? Let me cite just a few ways:

First, there is peace. Nothing characterizes the realities of our day better than the words "rift" and "restlessness." Peace with God, peace with men, and peace with ourselves are among our greatest needs. It is a rare thing to see such peace manifested, but if you want to see it, look for a godly man or woman— especially one who is in the autumn of life.

I have ceased counting the occasions when I have been at the bedside of an older person who knows that there is little time left, yet who has great peace. And I don't know how many times I have been with older persons whose arthritic limbs have been racked with pain, but who, nevertheless, had an inner harmony that transcended it. There is every reason for despair and complaining, but like the men and women of Bunyan's land of Beulah, there is a calmness and a confidence about them that is simply not affected by the winds of strife that usually toss people about.

Then, there is patience. There is something about the experiences of a lifetime—the strains, the struggles, the suffering, and through it all, the years of depending upon God's mercies—that bring the grace of patience to fruition in old age. And what a testimony and what encouragement such patience is!

Then, there is praise. Praise, says John Drescher, is joy's twin. It is joy's outward expression. "Joy is pressure in the system, while praise is the safety valve letting go."[3]

Like peace and patience, praise is a fruit seen in Christians of all ages. But again, there is something especially beautiful about the man or the woman who has spent a lifetime serving God, and still has a cup of joy overflowing with praise! What a testimony and encouragement that is!

So, then, this is the fruitfulness of which the Bible speaks, a fruitfulness that flourishes even though the body is declining, a fruitfulness which makes old age something to look forward to after all, which makes the autumn of life a welcome friend, too.

[1]Emily Dickinson, #12 in *The Complete Poems of Emily Dickinson,* ed. Thomas H. Johnson (Boston: Little, Brown, and Company), p. 11.

[2]From *The Kokinshu,* trans. Arthur Waley, *Anthology of Japanese Literature,* ed. Donald Keene (New York: Grove Press, 1955), p. 77.

[3]John Drescher, *Spirit Fruit* (Scottdale, Pennsylvania: Herald Press, 1974), p. 115.

It's difficult to believe in a resurrection from the dead in a scientific age. And even for those of us who do, this present life, nevertheless, seems to be the one making the greatest impact.

8

I Like It Here

M. T. Brackbill, who taught for years at my alma mater, wrote a poem of praise which he began and ended with the words, "Lord, I like it here."

Those are words that most of us can echo: "Lord, I like it here." But I suspect that most of us would like to linger on those words a little longer than M. T. Brackbill would have. "Lord, I *like* it here," we'd say, and we'd mean, "Here is where I want to stay! Lord, I like it *here!*"

It's okay for the apostle Paul to say that he "would prefer to be away from the body and at home with the Lord" (2 Cor. 5:8). As for us—well, we believe there's a heaven—we have our sights set for there—we think of this earth as an inn on our way to the heavenly Jerusalem. But on our honest days, we must admit that we like to put our emphasis on the *here*. "Lord, I like it *here.*"

Sure, the world has its problems, its heartaches, and

its headaches, but the good outweighs the bad—doesn't it? Sure, there's war, and tyranny, and disease, and famine. But we're at peace right now, and we're making progress on all these other things—aren't we? Even if the progress *is* a bit slow, there is always something to smile about—isn't there?

Well, that all depends on whom you talk to. Would Job, in the midst of his troubles, have thought so? Shaken by the loss of possessions, family, health . . . suffering continually, and tormented by his friends, would Job have agreed that the good outweighs the bad, or that there is always something to smile about?

Or take the slaves sold at auction during the last century in the United States. Terms: one-third cash, the remainder by interest-bearing bonds. So reads the advertisement for one sale in Savannah. How about it? Would these slaves have agreed that the good in the world outweighs the bad?

Or take the Jews who suffocated in the gas chambers of the Third Reich or those who were buried alive. Or the millions killed by Mao Tse-tung's people's army in their march to victory over Chiang Kaishek. Or the starving children of India and the sub-Sahara. Or the patients in cancer wards. Would they agree that the good outweighs the bad? Would their song be, "I like it here"?

No, for Job, man, born of woman, was of few days and full of trouble. The New York *Tribune* described the sale of those Savannah slaves as a tragic affair, with the faces of those who stepped up on the block as always telling of "more anguish than it is in the power of words to express." For the Jews murdered by Hitler, the Chinese slaughtered by Mao, the starving children of overpopulated and underproductive lands, and the disease-ravaged patients of terminal wards, the answer is likewise, "I do *not* like it here!" Life for them is a nightmare from which only kind death offers an escape.

Our answer is different only because we are part of a privileged minority in the world . . . more privileged than we imagine, more of a minority than we imagine.

What's Really Important?

In First Thessalonians 4, the apostle Paul gives us a brighter picture:

> Brothers, we do not want you to be ignorant about those who fall asleep, or to grieve like the rest of men, who have no hope. We believe that Jesus died and rose again and so we believe that God will bring with Jesus those who have fallen asleep in him (vv. 13-14).

But how much does that impress us—really? It's difficult to believe in a resurrection from the dead in a scientific age. And even for those of us who do, this present life, nevertheless, seems to be the one making the greatest impact.

For example, do you, even if you believe what the Bible says about the resurrection from the dead, act as though that were the most important news about your life?

How was it with you this morning? Did you wake with the consciousness that you are headed for a brand-new day and a brand-new lease on life? Did you spring out of bed with a tingling feeling of that growing seed of new life that is within you, because of the fact that you've put your trust in Jesus Christ? Or was the only Life you were aware of this morning in your cereal bowl?

65

It's quite likely that you never once gave a thought —not even a passing thought—to the resurrection from the dead when you woke up from your sleep this morning. As Helmut Thielicke has put it, we just don't think that way: "The bird of a cheerful breakfast in the hand is worth more than a couple of resurrections in the bush."

No, if we give any thought to the resurrection from the dead at all, it is probably at Easter. On Easter we are conditioned to think about it. It is a kind of parenthesis, out of touch with ordinary life the rest of the year.

Or if we have a close brush with death, or if we're in the twilight years of our life—then we might give an occasional moment to thinking about the resurrection from the dead. Even then, however, we're likely to remind the Lord that there are a few things we want to do yet, and that we rather like it here!

Isn't it interesting that when old age comes, and death is no longer the abstraction it once was, or when we're in some circumstance that suddenly brings home its reality to us, we still push off the resurrection?

When we think about Jesus, which do we give more thought to? His resurrection, or the example He left us—His perfect character and the moral principles He taught?

The Focus of the New Testament

But which is most important in the New Testament? The New Testament's focus is not upon the character of Jesus, nor the example of Jesus, but rather upon His death and resurrection! Apart from that miraculous fact, there would be no New Testament, there would be no church, there would be no Christian faith, and there would be no hope for either those who can or cannot say of the world, "I like it here."

If there is no hope of resurrection, what do I say to those who are in bondage to the fear of death?

But because Jesus died and rose again, I do have something to say. I can say to those who are growing old, to those who are terminally ill, to those who are starving, to those who are grieving, that God has been there! He's been there in the darkness, in the despair, in the loneliness, in the death—and all is well!

And I can say something more. The great fact of the resurrection has something to say about the love of God here and now, too. If God has a love for any of these suffering ones in His heart, that love is absolutely meaningless apart from the hope that something is better beyond death. A taste of this can be had even now, when Jesus comes into a man's or a woman's heart. A taste of it can be had even now if Christians will demonstrate something of the better day through kind and loving acts.

In a sense the hope of the resurrection from the dead speaks most eloquently to those who have never been able to say, "I like it here."

I, for one, like it here; but I'm going to like it there a lot more.

Worry comes from an Anglo-Saxon word meaning to strangle. In a sense, many people do choke to death from worry. Such diseases as high blood pressure, nervous breakdowns, and ulcers have been traced to worry.

9

One Day at a Time

One of the well-known gospel songs has the words, "one day at a time, sweet Jesus." That's good advice if we'll take it. Jesus put it a bit differently, but the same thought was clearly there when He said, "Do not worry about tomorrow, for tomorrow will worry about itself. Each day has enough trouble of its own" (Matt. 6:34).

Yet, in our obsession to know what tomorrow holds and in our need to somehow control our futures, we often squander with worry the precious minutes God has given us today. An American urged his Oriental friend to run in order to catch a subway train that was pulling into Park Street station in Boston. Hurriedly they deposited their tokens in the turnstile, raced along the crowded platform, and squeezed into the train just as the doors were closing. "Whew! That was close," said the American. "The next train won't pass through for another five minutes."

His friend looked puzzled, then asked him, "And

what, my brother, do you intend to do with the five minutes you saved?"

It's true! More often than we realize, we allow the future to crowd in on the present so that we miss the blessings God wants to give us right now. Anticipation is healthy, but apprehension consumes us. In our zeal to preserve an uncertain tomorrow, we end up wasting the gift of an unspoiled today.

Do you remember the story of the man whose jet arrived late on the evening of an important speaking engagement? Racing O. J. Simpson style through the terminal and into a waiting taxi, he had one thing on his mind—somehow he had to make up for lost time. "Step on it! Quick!" he said to the cab driver. The taxi peeled out and fifteen minutes later was still racing down streets and skidding around corners. Finally, the man said to the cabby, "How much farther is it?" And the cabby replied, "I don't know, sir; you haven't told me where you want to go!"

That's us (too often!). We are like Stephen Leacock's famous rider, who "flung himself upon his horse and rode off madly in all directions." We are frantically on the move, but our progress from "A" to "B" is by the most circuitous route imaginable. Edna St. Vincent Millay said it for us all: "Life must go on, but I forget just why."

There is a sense, I suppose, in which our fretful ways are a natural thing. We *are* incredibly vulnerable creatures when you think of it. And we *don't* really have much to say about the future. Retirement policies, insurance plans, emergency savings accounts, and a retired mortgage are fine, but even with all those forms of security and more, we nevertheless feel understandably exposed and anxious.

What's ahead for me? Am I going to get old and senile? Is my business going to sink in the next economic slump? Am I going to get Legionnaires disease at my meeting in the Garment District? Is my jet going to collide with some private plane? Are the Russians planning a secret attack? No wonder Auden called this "the age of anxiety."

However, the truth is that every age is an "age of anxiety." Take the day in which Jesus lived. Why else would he speak of not worrying about tomorrow? What other reason could there have been when, as we're told in Mark 4:19, He spoke of "the worries of this life"? And do you remember His words to Martha? "Martha, Martha, you are worried and upset about many things" (Luke 10:41).

Two Kinds of Fear

There are two kinds of fear—normal fear and abnormal fear. Normal fear is an emotion given to us by God for our benefit and our protection. Unlike abnormal fear, normal fear is a healthy respect for danger rather than an obsessive terror of it.

Abnormal fear, however, is a kind of bondage (Heb. 2:15) that tears at our emotional stability for all of our lives. Abnormal fear is a persistent and unrealistic fear of a situation or object.

Such fears are often called phobias. For example, agoraphobia is the fear of being in a large, open space; claustrophobia is the fear of a confined space; aichmophobia is the fear of knives or other sharp or pointed tools; microphobia is the fear of germs; nychtophobia, of night; astraphobia, of thunderstorms—and there are many, many more.

Worry Is Abnormal Fear

Worry is abnormal fear. The word comes from an Anglo-Saxon word meaning to strangle. And in a sense, many people do choke to death from worry. Many maladies and diseases, among them, high blood pressure, nervous breakdowns, heart attacks, and ulcers, have been traced to worry. As someone once said about ulcers, "It's not what you eat, it's what eats you."

So, worry affects not only the mind but the body. In fact, research has shown that as many as one in four who visit a physician have symptoms brought on by the tension and strain of worry. Most doctors would agree with Mahatma Gandhi, who said that there is nothing which wastes away the body like worry.

Because worry robs us of the blessings of each day and even the blessing of good health, it's easy to understand why Jesus warned us not to worry about tomorrow. But is it possible? Can we really be freed from the bondage of worry?

The apostle Paul thought so. "For God did not give us a spirit of timidity," he wrote, "but a spirit of power, of love and of self-discipline" (2 Tim. 1:7). The apostle Paul had more to fear than most men. Because of his fervent zeal to spread the Good News, he was stoned, beaten, mobbed, thrown into prison, even shipwrecked. Still he kept on, and he did not worry.

That's how it was with Jesus, too. He didn't just talk about not worrying; He demonstrated it. When caught in a violent storm on Lake Galilee, the disciples became terrified. But Jesus napped in the back of the boat.

Jesus and Paul knew how to live "one day at a time." They demonstrated that we don't need to be slaves to worry, that we can be free from fear about tomorrow.

71

But how do we do that? How do we learn to live "one day at a time"? How do we keep from being the kind of pessimistic souls whose birds are all ravens and whose food is all carcinogenic? Let me suggest a simple, but I trust not simplistic, solution. First, we need a new perspective. Second, we need a new priority.

A New Perspective

Several things should be included in this new perspective. The first grows out of a consideration of what Jesus says in verses 19 and 20 of Matthew 6: "Do not store up for yourselves treasures on earth, where moth and rust destroy, and where thieves break in and steal. But store up for yourselves treasures in heaven, where moth and rust do not destroy, and where thieves do not break in and steal." In other words, all the "things" we are so preoccupied with in life are passing—they are transient. All the "things" we worry so much about have a characteristic flaw: they don't last. All the things we think are going to give us the security we long for, evaporate. Like a meteor they flash before our eyes in dazzling fashion. But even as they streak across the horizon in their blaze of glory, they are burning up. In the end all that's left of them is scattered ashes.

For the most part, then, the future we worry about is a future full of nothings. In Garfield's speech on the assassination of Lincoln, he spoke of "the security of the future." But there is no future at all, except for God's future. The "flight of future days" is such that, like the pot of gold at the end of the rainbow, it can never be had—only sought. Like the mechanical rabbit the greyhound chases around the racetrack, a future filled with corruptible things is always just out of reach. You grab for it and it vanishes. The oasis in the distance

72

always turns out to be a mirage, and despite your frantic efforts your thirst only becomes more acute. You think that you are going to find security in a family, but what happens when one of your family dies? You think it's going to be obtained by accumulating wealth, but what happens when *you* die? You think security lies in getting to the top, but what happens when you get there and you find you're all alone?

We need the realization that "things" just don't measure up to our needs because they are not eternal. They are only temporary trinkets.

The second part of the new perspective we need is the realization that the things we worry so much about are not productive to our spiritual growth. As Jesus put it in Matthew 6:32, they are things that pagans run after. God takes care of all our earthly needs, but the pagan mentality is afraid to trust Him for them.

I need to take a good many airplane flights in the course of a year. Suppose when we hit some bumpy air on one of them, I express my alarm to the flight attendant, complaining that the captain should fly around such turbulence. Suppose the flight attendant reports back to me a few minutes later that the captain says I may fly the plane myself if I've a mind to. Whose ability will I trust? The captain's or my own? (I can't even fly a paper airplane!) Just so, God takes care of our everyday needs as a matter of course.

Finally, we need to realize the importance of focusing only on those things which are acceptable in God's sight, namely, His kingdom and its righteousness.

Perhaps we can summarize the new perspective by saying that it is foolish to worry about anything that doesn't measure up to heaven's E.P.A. requirements. If it's not *eternal*, it's not worth worrying about. If it's not spiritually *productive,* it's not worth worrying about. If it's not *acceptable* (or, in other words, worthy) in God's sight, then it's not worth worrying about.

A New Priority

How do we come by this new perspective? How do we decide what's worth being anxious about? We do so in this way—by laying hold of a new priority, the priority of God's kingship. "But seek first his kingdom and its righteousness," Jesus says, "and all these things will be given to you as well" (Matt. 6:33).

What does that mean? Well, in summary form it means that we need to be concerned with God first, and not ourselves. Ultimately, all our anxieties are centered around *ourselves* and *our* peace of mind. We become anxious about food and clothing and security and the future, because we think those are the most important things in our lives. But when, instead, the kingdom of God is the most important thing in our lives, when His rule and His righteousness are first, then all that changes. When we begin to realize that we are the children of God and heirs of eternity, then all the things about which we've been so anxious in the past take on a secondary importance.

Serving God comes first. We trust Him to take care of the secondary needs, and He does. So, because our first priority has become serving God and not looking out for ourselves, our perspective on the things that formerly worried us changes. When we are our own masters, we need to worry about providing for ourselves. However, when God is our Master, our daily provisions become His responsibility. We must do our part, but any worrying is to be centered on serving Him and being His man or woman.

74

Seeking God's kingdom first involves devoting these three things to God: our days; our energies; and our lives.

Our Days

Every day needs to begin with God. "Anxiety," someone has said, "is the measure of the distance between man and God." When God comes, anxiety goes; when anxiety comes, God goes. As Jesus puts it in Matthew 6: "No one can serve two masters." The way to close the distance between you and God is to seek Him early, to set aside a time with Him as the very first business of your day. If the kingdom comes first in your life, it means that God must come first, for the phrase "kingdom of God" literally means the rule of God, and God cannot be separated from His rule. If God is going to reign in your life, then you have to spend time with Him. You have to seek Him early. Your relationship with Him comes before everything else. That is central. And when that relationship is intact, then every other relationship is toned up. If that relationship is loose, then every other relationship goes loose with it. If you are in daily touch with God, then anxiety will largely disappear as well. If you have a quiet time, you will have a quiet heart. If you have a quiet heart, then you will have peace. So, God must be first in your day.

Our Energies

He must also be first in the directing of our energies. Most men and women in our society give their strength to worldly pursuits, and their weakness to their religion. They are completely with it during the money-making hours of their weeks, but when it comes to prayer and Bible reading they are out of it. During the week, they're looking for all the overtime they can get; but when it comes to church, they must be out exactly on the stroke of the hour or they are distressed.

Why can't we get as excited about spiritual things? Why must it be that self has our energies and Jesus has our lukewarmness? Why can't our enthusiasm be for the best of causes and the best of Masters, instead of for trivial things that do not last, that do not produce spiritual fruit, and that are not acceptable to God?

God has given His best, His crucified Son! Why can't we give Him our best? It's sad but the comparative sizes of the Bible and the ledger are symbolic, I think, of our allegiances. But it doesn't need to be that way! If we really want it, first things can be first in our lives! So, if it's as true for you as it has sometimes been for me, that your Christianity is on vacation, why not begin right now to direct your energies into not just talking about Christ, but living Him!

Our Lives

But in addition to devoting our days and our energies to God, we need to go that final step and devote our entire lives to Him. Every step away from God wastes three steps: one in going away, one in coming back, and the one you could have been taking. All too often we are in retreat, backing away from God's new challenges to us. We know that He ought to have complete control and be at the helm of our lives. We know that only when we're closing the gap between ourselves and Him are we closing the gap on worry. We know that we need to be men and women of God first, and *then* teachers and homemakers and laborers and farmers and secretaries and nurses. We know that we have to be Christians first, then Americans—that our national citizenship is subservient to our heavenly and our universal citizenship. We know that the order in everything must be "Christ first," and everything else afterwards. And we know that when that is true, we need be anxious about nothing in life! We know it; why don't we act on it? Our God is able to supply every one of the needs we are so uncertain about, if we will just rest in Him day by day, trust in Him for the needs of the hour, depend on Him to keep us safe and secure. He supplies life abundantly, such as we never dreamed possible.

So, does worry empty tomorrow of its trouble? No, rather it empties today of its strength. We *will* have the strength to bear troubles when they come, but it will not be through investments, pensions, elaborate schemes, or nest eggs; rather, it will be through the One who gives us the water and bread of life "one day at a time."

☆ ☆ ☆ ☆ ☆ ☆ ☆ ☆ ☆ ☆

TRADE IN OLD HABITS

☆ ☆ ☆ ☆ ☆ ☆ ☆ ☆ ☆ ☆

You've tried diets; you know that no diet is enough. You've tried exercise; you know that no exercise program is enough. You've tried starvation; you know that starvation is too much. What do you try next?

10

Enough Is Enough

The chief cause of overweight is overeating. There was a time when it was called gluttony, but today we use tamer terms and speak of overeating or overindulgence or excessive appetites. There was also a time when it was spoken of as sin, but today we think of it merely as a problem.

Serious Business

However, sometimes kinder words can really be an unkindness. We may think we are being helpful by toning "gluttony" down to "overeating," and "sin" down to a "problem." In reality we may be causing persons to take lightly something that is very serious indeed. Certainly the Bible takes gluttony to be sin. Paul says that those whose stomach is their god are on their way to destruction (Phil. 3:19). From the earliest times, then, the church has thought of gluttony as a deadly sin.

Isolation from Friends and God

Not only is the glutton on his way to destruction, he is also on his way to painful isolation. It is no secret that overweight persons are usually ostracized in our society. There is something embarrassing about being seen with someone who shovels instead of spoons and waddles instead of walks. "Watch a gluttonous man at his food," says Henry Fairlie. "He is like a hog at its swill. . . . He does not chew his meat but champs, chomps, crunches, and craunches. He crams, gorges, wolfs, and bolts." Who could blame anyone for wanting to avoid such a person?

Often, gluttony and laziness go together, which is another reason for avoidance. It is interesting to note that Titus 1:12 makes this connection: "Cretans are always liars, evil brutes, lazy gluttons." It is not blubber that slows the glutton down; rather, it's the fact that eating becomes a preoccupation and takes the glutton's attention away from more important matters. Think of the energy put into the feasts of ancient Rome, for example. Suetonius' favorite dish, he tells us, consisted of a mixture of the livers of pike, the brains of pheasants and peacocks, the tongues of flamingoes, and the milk of lampreys. These were brought by his captains and ships from the whole empire, from Parthia to the Spanish strait. Imagine the energy wasted in even thinking up such a ludicrous concoction, let alone obtaining the ingredients! Just so, today's glutton is so preoccupied with thinking about what he's going to eat at his next meal that everything else, including his duties, becomes secondary. This, too, contributes to his isolation, for what friends he has are quick to sense that even they play second fiddle to appetite.

The glutton also becomes more isolated from God. So important is his eating that thanking God for the blessing of daily bread never occurs to him; or if it does occur to him, it is the force of habit. As time goes on it becomes rushed and mechanical—it is not really thanks at all. To put it another way, God's daily provision is taken for granted. The table becomes the glutton's altar, his stomach his god. Provisions become more important than the Provider, and glutton and God grow farther and farther apart.

Gluttony Defined

In the thirteenth century, the Italian theologian, St. Thomas Aquinas, considered gluttony so grievous that he felt constrained to define it in detail. He said it involved eating too soon, too much, too fast, and too expensively. Had he said it this morning, he would have been just as right. Someone said, "Tell me what you eat and I'll tell you what you are." Is this really true? We know that it is too true.

Of course, gluttony is not merely a matter of food. Excessive drinking, for example, might well be placed in the same category. When Paul spoke of those whose god is appetite, we mustn't suppose that he meant food only. But food is probably the most important overindulgence with which you and I have to deal.

All this is not to say that Christianity doesn't believe in pleasure, that eating is taboo because it is an enjoyable activity. Some of the old Puritans were known to suggest such things, and some modern-day ascetics have, too. Christianity is not against pleasure and enjoyment, however. God made eating an enjoyable activity, and we ought to take pleasure in it. Remember, it is overeating—gluttony—that we are criticizing. Appetite is not evil; it is the abuse of appetite that is wrong. If you do not like eating, something is certainly lacking and I feel sorry for you. However, if you like your eating too much (even more than your food), then I feel even more sorry for you. "Every man," says the Bible, "should eat and drink and enjoy the fruit of his labor." But the Bible also says that the man who is enslaved by his stomach is on his way to destruction.

Well, what can you do if eating is an obsession? How do you free yourself from the slavery of appetite? You've tried diets. You know that no diet is enough. You've tried exercise; you know that no exercise program is enough. You've tried starvation; you know that starvation is too much. What do you try next?

The Set of the Mind

How about a new way of thinking? Let me quote from the passage in the Bible to which I've alluded several times. Here's what Paul has to say:

> For, as I have often told you before and now say again even with tears, many live as enemies of the cross of Christ. Their destiny is destruction, their god is their stomach, and their glory is in their shame. Their mind is on earthly things. But our citizenship is in heaven (Phil. 3:18-20).

Do you see what Paul suggests the difference is? He doesn't say anything about calories at all, does he? He doesn't say anything about push-ups either, though both calories and push-ups are important. Rather, the difference Paul sees is a difference of attitudes, a difference in thinking, a difference of affections. The group of people whose appetite is god have their affections, their minds, set on earthly things. But the group of people with whom Paul identifies are thinking, instead, about heaven and how God would have them to live. Their hunger is not for food but for righteousness. Their priority is not their stomachs but their Creator. Could that really be the key to overcoming the sin of gluttony?

Five Steps to a Solution

Let me suggest several things I think will be helpful to you if you have this problem:

First, admit you have the problem. As a pastor, the first thing I try to do in my counseling is to get people to face up to the fact that they have a problem. Sometimes that is half the battle.

Second, determine to start dealing with the problem today. Not tomorrow. Not next week. Not next month. Not after the party you're going to next Friday night. Not after the family reunion that's coming up. But today—right now.

Third, set your mind on the things of heaven. Decide that you are going to find your satisfaction in life, not in eating, but in living for God. Don't hunger for food, but for righteousness. You say, "How can I do that?" Well, it's not easy. You can't do it unless you are relying on God to give you strength. So trust Him to help you. Ask Him for His help. If you are serious about your problem, He's going to be serious about helping you.

Fourth, do those things you know you need to do. Cut down on your food intake. Eat deliberately, not out of compulsion. Eat to live instead of living to eat. Eat out of need rather than out of want. And exercise! Cutting down on the bread and cheese is not enough. Exercise! Not only is it good for your heart, but it helps you to burn up calories that would otherwise turn into fat.

Consult your doctor first, of course, so that you know what kind of regimen you can handle. But don't neglect this very important way to good health.

Finally, keep a log. Evaluate your eating habits each day. When you've overindulged, confess your sin to God and ask His help in not repeating your mistake tomorrow. If you don't log what you've eaten, you will find it very difficult to break the habit of overeating. Remember, too, that habits are not broken overnight. They must be worked on day by day. That's a second reason for keeping a daily log of what you eat.

I suppose there are other good pointers I could mention, but these, I think, are the most essential ones. Especially important, however, is the need to rely upon God to satisfy you. Do that, and the first thing you know, you'll be able to wear belts with your dresses, tuck in your shirttails again, get rid of the pleated pants and baggy sweaters—and, best of all, discover the joy and freedom of giving another part of your life over to God's control!

There is much truth in Robert Frost's
observation about willing people. He
said there are plenty of them in the
world, "some willing to work, the rest
willing to let them."

11

Life Without Cares

What have the following in common: laborers too union
happy to put in an honest day's work; shopkeepers too
fond of the old ways to compete; students involved in too
many extra-curriculars to study; and teachers too content with last year's outlines to keep up with the latest
scholarship? Their common denominator is that they've
all slipped into the pattern of taking the easy road. All
of them have succumbed to subtle forms of laziness.
Usually we think of laziness as something other people
struggle with, but all of us encounter just enough of it to
help us know the problem could be anyone's. And such
terms as *procrastination* and *lack of discipline* underline
the fact that the forms of laziness are many. It is both
subtle and varied in its manifestations. It is not something you are born with but something you drift into.
Most lazy people do not become that way by intent.

Just how do people slip into it? What's behind the
habit of pulling the covers over your head when the

alarm clock rings? What keeps people from adhering to a schedule? What makes them put off doing things until the last minute?

Causes of Laziness

Often laziness begins in childhood. If children don't learn to work when they're young, they will probably develop a pattern of avoidance that will be with them for a lifetime. Children ought not to be slaves, but they ought to have certain duties at home that teach them something about the importance of work—its wholesomeness, its dignity, its necessity. Children need to develop a sense of responsibility early if they are to become disciplined adults. Age three or four is not too young.

Laziness also has a direct relationship to apathy. Laziness begins in the mind. It is an attitude that says: "I don't care; I don't want to know; don't bother me and I won't bother you; don't rock the boat; let's do it the way we've always done it." It is an attitude that is content to flow with the tide. It is content with get-rich-quick schemes, self-help gimmicks, and the avoidance of pain, difficulty, or sorrow. It chooses laxness over vigilance, acceptance over decision, timidity over speaking out, observation over participation, mass production over craftsmanship, instant over home-made, and denial over facing reality.

This attitude is epidemic in the Western world. It accounts for a host of modern ills—from the individualism that makes us nations of strangers, to the TV tyranny that makes us families of strangers. For many, even work itself takes on the goal of not having to work someday. Their attitude toward work is that of the little boy who described it as something other people think of for you, while play is something you think of for yourself. Their goal is a life without cares.

The Pervasiveness of the Attitude

So, there's much truth in an observation Robert Frost once made. He said there are plenty of willing people in the world, "some willing to work—the rest willing to let them." Jerome K. Jerome confirmed Frost's thought when he quipped, "I love work; I can sit and watch it for hours." But there are many who confirm it even more potently than he, who are not humorists but actual practitioners in the art of sideline squatting. Like this man's, their epitaph might well read:

> He slept beneath the moon,
> He lived beneath the sun:
> And lived a life of going-to-do
> And died with nothing done.

Even in the realm of religion, laziness has its effect. It despises the legitimate use of the intellect, for example, and glorifies habit in the name of faith. It disowns God's great gift of the mind, refusing to accept the legitimacy of a faith thought out. This is tragic. Not only does it do great harm to the credibility of the Christian church, but it results in the emergence of a spineless pseudo-Christianity that preaches not the life of discipleship but the gospel of materialism, and cannot even say *what* it believes, let alone *why*.

We are used to hearing folks bemoan the advent of shorter work weeks, bigger welfare checks, and energy-consuming conveniences. But the inclination toward laziness has even broader ramifications than those for our society. It raises the whole question of where our priorities are, as well. Some time back a

British doctor, discussing the whole problem of work and wages, said that what is happening in our time is that no one works for the sake of getting things done anymore. Doctors no longer practice medicine primarily to relieve suffering, but to make a living—the cure of the patient is merely something that happens as a part of the process. I know of at least two magazines for dentists that suggest it's true in that profession, too. Neither of the magazines is interested at all in clinical or scientific material. Rather, they are directed to the business side of dentistry. Likewise, in the legal profession it is not uncommon for lawyers to accept briefs on the basis of the remuneration rather than because they have a passion to see justice done. One begins to wonder if there is anyone anymore who takes an occupation for the sake of making the world a better place, rather than for the sake of the pay.

There's a story about William Carey which I think illustrates this, because whenever I tell it, there are always a few who find it rather corny and anachronistic. One day a friend came to Carey and said, "I want to speak to you very seriously. By spending so much time preaching, you are neglecting your business. If you would tend your business better, you would prosper more."

Carey's reply was: "Preaching *is* my business. I cobble shoes only to pay the expenses."

Consequences

Not long ago, a friend asked me, "We hear a lot about the Biblical command to rest on the seventh day, but why doesn't anyone remember we're also commanded to work the other six days?"

I replied that there are plenty of people struggling on

both sides of that question—that while there are plenty of lazy people in the world, there are also plenty of workaholics.

"In fact, I know a few personally," I said. "They practically live at the office, and even when they're at home, they're mentally at work."

But in the end I also had to concede that my friend had a point. There are too many in our society who feel the world owes them a living, and many more (including many Christians) who are aware of the Bible's insistent emphasis on the importance of work but who are unable to overcome their habitual laziness.

Probably the Book of Proverbs is hardest on such persons. For instance, it warns that lazy people will go hungry and that their laziness will be their undoing (19:15). In another place it adds that the lazy man's cravings will be the death of him (21:25). Again, in Proverbs 24:33-34, the warning is: "A little sleep, a little slumber, a little folding of the hands to rest—and poverty will come on you like a bandit and scarcity like an armed man."

But the problems in Proverbs aren't the only ones such persons will encounter. It's true that the lazy man or woman will have less to eat, little prospect of keeping things together, and the possibility of an early death. But there are other pitfalls, too.

Think of what apathy alone can do. Robert Mc-Cracken said of it, "Anger slays its thousands and apathy slays its ten thousands." He was right. When apathy gets hold of you, you have no goals, no ambitions, no purpose. When apathy gets hold of you, you are doomed; your mind begins to deteriorate, and so does your body.

All laziness in fact is atrophic; it wastes you away.

When laziness of any sort gets hold of you, you lose. The lazy student not only fails to make the honor roll, but he will probably fail to get the job he wants. The lazy community will scare away businesses and industry, and will find its buildings deteriorating, its parks becoming eyesores, and even its people degenerating. Laziness keeps the hobo from respectability, the prostitute from purity, and the thief from honesty.

Procrastination is a particularly harmful form of laziness. And it's perhaps the most common. Its harmfulness has been illustrated by the story of the farmer who noticed some algae forming on his pond. He wasn't concerned, however, since most of the pond was uncovered by it. Even when he became aware that the algae was doubling each night, he remained unconcerned. One day the man noticed that the algae now covered half the pond, so he determined to do something about it the next day. But, of course, by then, the whole pond was covered.

What Can Be Done?

It is a distressing thing to discover that you're in bondage to laziness. You may call it "lack of discipline" or "the habit of putting things off," but that does not make it easier. You may have learned to rationalize your non-achievements, but that doesn't help either. The loss of dignity and hope comes just the same. A Christian ought not to be a slave to laziness, you tell yourself. A Christian ought to have victory. But the hard fact is, you don't have victory!

What can you do?

For one thing, you can accept laziness for what it is. Basically, it involves *habit* and *attitude*. Bad habits, even with God's help, are usually overcome one day at a time. God sometimes helps us break bad habits overnight, but usually it takes longer, which I believe is for the purpose of teaching us to trust Him day by day. Wrong attitudes are overcome by spending time in the presence of persons whose attitudes are more wholesome than our own. I recommend spending time with God each day, therefore, and spending time in the Bible, His Word.

Second, you can enlist the help of a close friend or two. They cannot only give you much-needed prayer support and counsel, but they can evaluate your progress and be advocates to whom you have a certain accountability. And accountability is a great asset in developing new behavior patterns.

Third, carefully plan your activities and set goals. Goals and a schedule are essential. Also essential is a day-by-day evaluation of how well you meet them and keep them.

But above all, remember that only by God's help (His *daily* help) are you likely to succeed in finding freedom from the tyranny of habitual laziness.

Talk about misers and skinflints may leave you feeling untouched. But if you're like me, when you examine this one a bit more closely, you can't get off the hook quite as easily as you thought.

12

Possessed by Possessions

Do you remember the stories of Scrooge and King Midas you heard in your youth? Or the poem about the king in his counting house, counting out his money? The miser was always an old guy who sat at a table running his hands through a pile of coins. But most misers aren't like that at all. The misers in children's yarns are quite different from the misers of the real world. For one thing, the misers of the real world usually occupy themselves with spending money rather than counting it.

But that doesn't make sense, you say. A miser by definition is one who hoards his money. No—a miser by definition is one who loves to possess things. It may be coins . . . then, again, it may be an outlandish collection of fashions, a house full of antique furnishings, or even the biggest engagement rock on the block.

Philip Slater tells an interesting story about a certain wealthy neighborhood in his city. A few years ago drought struck the city, and water restrictions were imposed. The public responded magnificently. Even before emergency restrictions were put into effect, public consumption of water was down nearly 20 percent. In that one wealthy neighborhood, however, it was not down. There, water consumption went up—50 percent! That is a classic case of wealth addiction. It's not just the hoarding of *money*, but taking more than your share of *any* commodity.

There's an interesting footnote to this story, incidentally. When the greediness of this wealthy neighborhood became public knowledge, there was no public outcry at all! Slater says, "It seemed as if people *expected* the rich to take more than their share."

One wonders why. Could it be that the mentality of North Americans is such that even though most of us are not fabulously wealthy, we secretly wish we could be? Could it be that we have come to view hoarding as O.K., providing you can get away with it? Could it be that even though we view miserliness as an ugly thing, in reality we are closet addicts ourselves?

You may think you don't know any misers, because you haven't met anybody who is fond of eyeballing the treasures in his vault. But what of the guy who glories in the grandeur of his new, expensive automobile, or the gal who spends more money on her hairstyle than on the groceries? Don't they run their eyes over their prized possessions as jealously as any fairy tale miser runs his eyes over his gold?

What of the cults surrounding certain stores, certain labels, certain tastes in food? What of your friends who live in museums instead of homes, who drive collectors' items instead of cars, who wear costumes instead of clothes? They do not possess their possessions; their possessions possess them! No wonder the Bible speaks of those who pretend to be rich but have nothing (Prov. 13:7), for there is a sense in which the miser is the poorest man or woman of all.

Who Is Affected?

The traditional name for wealth addiction is avarice. Avarice describes excessive, unbridled desire for what other people can't have. That makes avarice ugly. Worse, avarice makes people ugly. It causes them to rob, cheat, murder, slander, and more. It does something terrible to the souls of even those whose addiction is mild. Notice the last three letters of the word: I-C-E, ice! That describes the selfish heart of a greedy person. When you trace avarice back to its root meaning, you find that it describes someone who is miserable and unhappy.

When we hear avarice described in that way, most of us tend to think of ourselves as untouched. Talk about stealing and cheating, misers and skinflints, and wanting what the Joneses can't have seems quite foreign to our experience. But when we examine this one a bit more closely, it's not as easy to get off the hook as we've thought. They call avarice the old man's disease, but we get infected, too. That is why we think it humorous instead of sad when one of the world's wealthiest men is so stingy he has a pay phone installed in his home. That is why we're not surprised at a Hetty Green stuffing her clothes with newspapers to keep warm, while making a million dollars on the stock market.

Or think of the more direct manifestations of avarice in our lives. Take security, for example. What causes people to overinsure themselves? Why do we insist on unmerited job security? What compulsion always pushes us to get everything we can get, to put our faith in grabbing rather than in God? What possesses us to live as if we're alone in the world, building our own little fortresses, creating safe little worlds we can control? We vainly imagine we can get along just fine without others and without God.

Or take popularity. There are a lot of us for whom acceptance and prestige is an obsession. Just as some people crave money, we crave applause, recognition, honors. We love to be called by esteemed titles, or to have our names placed in yet another *Who's Who*.

Or take "keeping up with the Joneses." We may not have the means to do it on the grand scale of the wealthy, but how many times have we bought some item for ourselves or for our families because the neighbors had one (or because the neighbors didn't have one!)? That is when goods become gods, isn't it? And most of us have, at least on occasion, been guilty.

J. B. Chapman used to tell a story about going into a church in the dust bowl area during the depression of the early and middle Thirties. He had never seen such poverty. He inquired of the pastor as to what subject he should preach on. The pastor suggested that he use the text, "The love of money is the root of all evil." Chapman was astonished. "Why, the people are poorer here than anywhere I've been for a long, long time," he said. "Yes, that's probably true," said the pastor. "But the Bible doesn't say that it's the money that's the root of all evil. It is 'the love of money.' My people don't have money, but they sure do love it!"

Jesus was continually warning against the sin of avarice. He thought that the love of money was one of the most dangerous enemies of the well-being of the soul. And listen to words like these, which Jesus spoke: "Blessed are you who are poor, for yours is the kingdom of God. Woe to you who are rich, for you have already received your comfort" (Luke 6:20, 24). What must people have made of statements like those? Or take this one: "How hard it is for the rich to enter the kingdom of God! Indeed, it is easier for a camel to go through the eye of a needle than for a rich man to enter the kingdom of God" (Luke 18:24-25).

The Way to Right Attitudes

Well, that brings us to the question of the hour: How can we subdue and conquer this giant of avarice, which apparently affects those of modest means just as much as the wealthy? Jesus said that the answer lies in wanting more, not less. It consists in wanting just as much of certain things as you can get, except that those things are not things that money can buy. It involves accumulating certain things for your own—as much as you can, as fast as you can—it involves new priorities. But they are spiritual priorities, not material or intellectual.

To begin with, we are to love God with all our heart, soul, mind, and strength, and we are to love our neighbor as ourselves. We are not to love money, but mankind. We are not to love goods, but God. In fact, we are to love those two things so much that we shall be willing to take up our cross, just as He did, and sacrifice everything, if need be—just as He did.

Some say avarice is an old man's disease. It's not, but it makes you old. Some say it's a disease of the wealthy. It is, but it is a disease of poorer folks, too. However, in Canada and the United States, how many poor are there? Compared to the rest of the world, we are very rich indeed!

The time to deal with jealousy is not when it finally gets to the destructive stage, where it wants to destroy something or someone. The time to deal with it is the time of its discovery.

13

Old Green Eyes

I once heard jealousy compared with a South American vine called the "matador." The vine grows up the trunk of a tree, ultimately choking and killing the tree. When it reaches the top of the tree, it crowns itself with a flower.

"'Matador' means 'killer,'" said the person making the comparison, "and jealousy is a killer, too. It kills the very best in us—our joy, our self-respect, our ability to love. At first it seems harmless enough, like the tiny matador vine at the foot of the tree; but if it is allowed to grow, it becomes an ugly thing indeed."

It's no wonder, then, that jealousy has been categorically condemned in almost every attempt to define it over the years. It's "a coal come hissing hot from hell," said Philip Bailey. "It is the mark of a jaundiced soul," said another. "It's a snake," said someone else.

The Destructiveness of Jealousy

Most of us associate the color green with jealousy. I suppose that goes back to Shakespeare's description of it as "green-eyed" in *The Merchant of Venice*. But while we probably consider that and all such descriptions to be overstatements, none of us can shake the certainty that jealousy has no claim whatever to being a respectable or healthy emotional activity.

Language like "green-eyed" and a coal "hissing hot from hell" may be dated, but jealousy has no trouble whatever living up to the reputation it implies. Call it envy, resentment, covetousness—anything you wish. All the harsh words that have been spoken about any facet of it have been fully warranted. It has wrecked marriages, split churches, destroyed friendships, and even led to murder.

Look at what jealousy did to King Saul, for example. Saul became very fond of the young man, David, who had killed the Philistine giant, Goliath. Saul made David his right-hand man, and for a time there was genuine love between the two men. But as Saul became older and David's accomplishments mounted, the king gradually became more and more jealous of his friend. Finally Saul could not stand him any longer; he actually plotted to take David's life. Saul, who had at one time been the most admired, most revered man in all of Israel, had become one of the ugliest men in Israel because he had allowed himself to be consumed by jealousy.

One of the ancient Greeks is supposed to have killed himself through jealousy. A statue had been built to celebrate the achievements of one of the great champions of the public games. But the champion's chief rival became so jealous that he vowed to destroy the statue. Every night he went out and chiseled away at the foundation of the statue. Under the cover of darkness he hoped to weaken its foundation until it finally toppled. But, as the story goes, when the statue fell, it fell on him and killed him. The statue, thus, became the monument he had always wanted for himself, but it was a monument, not to his achievements, but to his invidiousness.

The time to deal with jealousy is not when it finally gets to the destructive stage, where it wants to destroy something or someone. The time to deal with it is the time of its discovery. Just the probable effects of jealousy on our health ought to convince us of that.

Famed physiologist John Hunter knew what such feelings could do: "The first scoundrel that gets me angry will kill me," he said. Some time later, at a medical meeting, some remarks were made that incensed him. Red-faced, he stood up and bitterly denounced the person who had made the statements. His anger caused such a contraction of blood vessels in his heart that he fell dead.[1]

The story is told by Dr. S. I. McMillen of a man who came into his office with his fourteen-year-old son. The father said, "I only came to get some more pills for my wife's colitis." Immediately the boy responded, "Well, Dad, who has Ma been colliding with now?" Was there any connection between the two—the colitis and the colliding? There easily could have been!

Frequently, the anger that is spawned by jealousy causes internal damage to the physical system through the excess release of acid substances. But even more ominous is the possibility that fits of jealousy may bring about an inability to think rationally which, in the end, can destroy the person. One of the examples that immediately comes to mind is that of Judas. Jealousy, in the end, does the most damage to the possessor himself. Jealousy always has a way of turning inward. Of course others are affected, too, but the self-inflicted toll is the heaviest.

The Remedy for Jealousy

Let me suggest several ways to work at jealousy. *First,* if you feel resentment and jealousy, ask yourself if, with a little effort, you couldn't improve your performance to possibly match that of the person you're jealous of. That is by no means the best or total solution. But sometimes we fail even to try.

Second, recognize that you have your own special worth. Accept yourself. Accept the very special gifts God has given you, however modest. Use those gifts, remembering that in God's book it is not the abilities that you have, but how you use what you have, that decides whether you are third-rate or first.

Third, do what Paul suggests in Philippians 2. Consider the welfare of the one you have begun to resent. You will be amazed at what a tonic that is and at the healing that will take place (Phil. 2:3-4).

Fourth, begin looking for good—whatever good you can find—in the other person, and try to find ways to affirm it. Instead of brooding about your own misfortune, begin rejoicing in the fortune of others. Thank God that He is working in the way that He is, and ask Him to find special avenues of fruitfulness in your life, too.

Fifth, if you still find that you can't shake your feelings of jealousy, take them to God. Confess them there, and renounce them. In his First Letter, John reminds us that if we will do that—confess our sin—God will bring healing and forgiveness (see also James 5:16). Recognize, in other words, that you need to rely on a strength outside yourself in order to conquer this killer. Recognize the eternal truth of what Paul once said, that "in Christ" we can be ready for anything!

Jealousy is like a weed. It thrives anywhere. No one escapes it altogether. It rages in the breast of the great and small, the educated and uneducated, the rich and poor, the old and young, the religious and the non-religious. It corrupts us all to some degree, but in Christ's strength, it can be overcome.

---

[1]S. I. McMillen, *None of These Diseases* (Fleming Revell, 1967), p. 69.

Well, then, did Jesus fail to live up to His own standards? Have those who claim to have victory over anger accomplished something that the Master couldn't? That's the kind of question we are faced with, it seems to me.

14

Good and Angry

According to the teaching of Jesus, Christians are supposed to follow the way of love. Jesus said that the greatest commandment is to love God with all your heart and your neighbor as yourself. Likewise, the apostle Paul described love as the supreme Christian quality, ranking above even faith and hope. No wonder, then, Jesus said that this is the mark by which men would know His disciples.

But, if all that is true, then what about anger? Can there be any place for anger in an economy marked by love unlimited? I know some Christians who say that there is not and that they have had victory over anger. But I have not. (I often internalize it, but I struggle with it just the same.) And to be perfectly frank, I doubt that they have really had victory over anger, as they claim. All of us get angry!

Even Jesus got angry. Certainly His life is our very best example of love and forgiveness in action: His love for the hopeless and impossible; His refusal to meet hate with hate; His willingness to go even to the cross out of His love for mankind. But we also read passages aplenty in the New Testament about times when Jesus blazed into a fierceness of anger and into stinging, blistering words that have burned across the centuries: "You snakes," He said. "You generation of vipers. . . ." "You whitewashed coffins. . . ." "You children of hell. . . ." I'm not sure how you feel about it, but those do not sound like very loving words to me! "Gentle Jesus, meek and mild"? Tell some of the Pharisees that! Tell the corrupt moneychangers in the temple!

Well, then, did Jesus fail to live up to His own standards? Have those who claim to have victory over anger been able to accomplish something that the Master couldn't? That's the kind of question we are faced with, it seems to me.

Anger Affects Our Reason

You know, it's not just the Bible that condemns anger. Anger has been considered an abomination of Christian and non-Christian alike down through the centuries. For one thing, when anger prevails, reason is almost always tossed aside. "Anger blows out the lamp of the mind," said Ingersoll, and there's a lot of truth to that. William Alger put it this way: "Men often make up in wrath what they want in reason." That is just another way of saying, as Cato did in ancient Greece, that when we get angry we close our eyes.

Anger Injures Our Cause

For another thing, anger injures our cause instead of helping it. It's like being intoxicated. You are hardly aware of it at the time but others are, and they are turned off by it. That is especially true when your anger grows out of some trivial irritation. And if we're honest with ourselves, we will have to admit that is often the way it works. We are hammering in a nail, and our thumb gets in the way. Someone in the church hurts us, and we take it out on the whole church. The traffic light goes green, and the driver in the car ahead is daydreaming and isn't even aware of it.

Anger Affects Our Health

Anger can also affect our health. Resentment and grudge-bearing that are not resolved quickly can lead to ulcers, nervous breakdowns, heart attacks, and other bodily ailments. As someone put it, in life's frog ponds we may be able to out-croak our fellows, but it might truthfully be written on all too many death certificates that the victims died of "grudgitis." Have you ever heard some red-faced and bitter person say, "I'm going to get even with so-and-so if it's the last thing I ever do"? Sometimes it really is the last thing he ever does!

But what about the anger of Jesus? And what about the anger of Paul? For example, remember how when the high priest, Ananias, had his attendants strike Paul in the mouth, Paul shouted back, "God will strike you, you whitewashed wall!" (Acts 23:3). Paul has an interesting statement in the fourth chapter of Ephesians, however, that may help us. He says, "In your anger do not sin: Do not let the sun go down while you are still angry, and do not give the devil a foothold" (Eph. 4:26-27). Obviously, Paul didn't consider anger to be sin. And apparently Jesus didn't either, because He was constantly rebuking persons like the corrupt moneychangers, hypocrites, those offending children, and so on. Paul's statement agrees with Jesus' life: You can be angry, yet without sinning.

When Anger Is Right

When you look at the whole picture, you also see that the anger of Jesus and Paul was a special kind of anger. It was not an anger that could be described as the opposite of love. But at the very root of the anger was love itself! Of course they were angry with man's inhumanity to man; of course they were angry with selfishness and hypocrisy! Those things deserve our wrath, too. It's impossible to love humanity and not hate inhumanness. It's impossible to love justice and not be angry when someone receives injustice. It's impossible to love peace and not hate war. It's impossible to love God and not be angry with the enemies of God. Well, isn't it?

Most of us probably ought to be more angry, in fact—not less angry. We ought to be angry because of the rat-infested slums some people have to live in. We ought to be angry at the senseless torching of city blocks by corporation landlords. We ought to be angry with the narcotics traffickers. We ought to be angry with the networks when they beam trash into our living rooms. We ought to be angry with corruption in the labor unions and in business.

When I traded in one of my cars a few years ago, the dealer tried to get me to falsify the mileage in return for a slightly better deal. I don't mind telling you, that made me angry. You've experienced things like that too, and they should have made you angry! However, the trouble is that while Jesus' anger was touched off by something that hurt others, too often ours is touched off by only that which hurts us, personally.

107

I think that's where the sin comes in, when our anger arises out of wounded pride or bad temper. And it doesn't take much for that to happen with most of us, does it? And even righteous anger (justified anger about evil conditions or injustice, for example) can become that if we're not careful. I am thinking of the anger that erupted into violence so often in the sixties. I am thinking of justified anger that degenerates into brooding, bitter hatred. When anger becomes that, it becomes sin—deadly sin.

So, may I encourage you to remember that there is a right and a wrong kind of anger. Righteous anger is legitimate and necessary, but it needs to be guided—guided by compassion and love. And love, as Paul said it, is patient and kind, not jealous or proud, not irritable or resentful, and rejoices in the right. Therefore, be angry—but don't sin in the process.

*Vance Havner used to remark that this
generation of Christians is a generation
of experts rather than examples, that we
have heard all the preachers, read all
the books, and think we know everything there is to know. We want to be
thought of as scholars, he said, brilliant rather than childlike.*

15

The One and Only

The trouble with pride is that while it is easy to spot in
others, it often goes undetected in oneself. A Carthu-
sian monk, so the story goes, was explaining some of the
distinguishing features of his order. "When it comes to
good works," he was saying, "we can't hold a candle
to the Benedictines; as to preaching, we are not in a
class with the Dominicans; the Jesuits are way ahead
of us in learning; but when it comes to humility, we're
tops!"

Most of us are like that, which is why both Jesus and
the apostle Paul said we need to examine our own lives
very carefully before making judgments about others!
Only when we have seen some of the same weaknesses
in ourselves will we be able to give correction in love.

But the question is, How? How do we detect the
problem of pride in our own lives; and how do we deal
with it?

First, how do we spot the problem of pride in our lives?

That's more difficult than we think. A Sunday school teacher was teaching her class the story Jesus told about the proud Pharisee and the penitent publican. In concluding the lesson, she counseled her students to thank the good Lord that they were not like the Pharisee!

In thinking about how we diagnose pride in ourselves, we should probably recognize that the word "pride" has a broader meaning in our society than the sense in which we are using it. When we talk about pride as a "problem," we are not talking about self-respect, or the satisfaction that comes when we have done a job well, or a legitimate sense of God-given worth. We are talking about self-centeredness, boasting, arrogance, a perverted sense of self-esteem. It is this other side of pride that we want to detect.

A second thing we need to recognize about this wrong kind of pride is that it takes more than one form. There is, for example, *the pride of position*. A person looks down on others because he or she is functioning in a role or in a class of society which is generally regarded as more important than other roles or classes. "It's all right to keep your head up," said a friend of mine to such a person one day, "but how about keeping your nose at a friendly level?"

Then, there is *intellectual pride*. The Bible teaches that we are to trust in the Lord with all our beings and not depend on our own understanding (Prov. 3:5). But the intellectually proud are not like that. As Billy Graham has often put it, "They like to put God in a test tube; and if He cannot be put in a test tube, they cannot accept Him." They have never really thought about the fact, you see, that people are finite, and are therefore limited in what they can understand about the universe. There are many windows of understanding on God's creation that they can open, but there are certain other facts (eternally critical facts!) that they cannot learn except by divine revelation such as we have in the Scriptures. It is sad that so few have realized, as Pascal did, that the greatest attainment of human reason is the realization that human reasoning is limited.

Then, there is *material pride*. Even though the Bible declares that God is the Giver of every good and perfect gift, many people act as though the gifts are more important than the Giver. What they can store up in terms of cash, comforts, and collectors' items takes a higher priority in their lives than God does.

Still another manifestation of pride is *spiritual pride*, which is probably the worst kind of all. Yet, it is prevalent in our day. Vance Havner used to remark that this generation of Christians is a generation of experts rather than examples, that we have heard all the preachers, read all the books, and think we know everything there is to know. We want to be thought of as scholars, he said, brilliant rather than childlike.

That, then, is one of the prerequisites for getting on top of the problem of pride—an acute awareness of the many forms that pride can take.

The Dangers

Seldom will we expend the effort to abandon a practice, unless we feel it is really harmful. So, besides considering the manifestations of pride, it is also worthwhile to consider the dangers.

The old theologians had no doubt whatever about the

111

dangers of pride. We say, "How can pride possibly be as harmful as some of the other things discussed in this book—like jealousy or laziness or gluttony?" But the old theologians thought of pride as more deadly than any of them. They considered it the deadliest of the seven deadly sins. Of all the threats to a Christian's proper walk with God, they felt pride was the greatest.

They were right! Pride is no matter to be taken lightly. Pride affects us right at the center of our being, because, first of all, by definition pride is putting ourselves on center stage in the place of God. Pride is the worst form of idolatry, because pride is the worship of one's self.

Furthermore, not only does pride relegate God to a minor place, it puts others there, too. The proud man sees himself as the hero, the actor in the major role, and everyone else as part of the supporting cast. Few others play roles of any import whatever; they are merely playing bit parts.

But beyond that, pride is dangerous because it distorts our vision. When God and others are relegated to minor roles in our lives and we are all-important, then obviously something is wrong with our perception. Reality has become distorted. We've become puffed up with self-importance. William Sangster told a story about a nurse who was so conceited that whenever she took the pulse of a male patient she subtracted five points to allow for the impact of her personality!

In one of Saroyan's stories there is a similar description of the distorted perspective of pride. An old man, who had but one string left on his cello, played that one string from morning till night. When his wife sheepishly pointed out that other cellists kept moving their fingers up and down, from one position to another, the old man stopped playing and looked at his wife with a smile of pity. "I might have expected that from you," he said. "Your hair is long, but your understanding is short. Of course other players keep moving their fingers. They are trying to find the right place. I have found it!" Perhaps our vision is not that distorted (I hope not!); nevertheless, most of us can remember instances when pride came bursting through with a brashness and blindness that still embarrasses us. Perhaps our pride manifests itself more subtly than that of the nurse and the old cellist, but the distortion is still there, and the danger is still real.

Pride not only results in our diminishing others, it results in those others turning away from us. When pride takes over, we're not the only ones building barriers; others are helping us! What's saddest of all, though, is the fact that pride creates a barrier that puts us out of touch with God. "Something there is that doesn't love a wall," said Robert Frost . . . and he was right. God doesn't love a wall. In fact, He stepped into human history in the Person of Christ to tear down the wall between man and Himself. But when pride takes over, we are busily engaged in building it right back up again. God wants to give His strength to our lives, but the blindness of pride says, "No." Instead, we do exactly what He warns us against. We eat; we build our houses; we raise our herds; we earn our money—then, instead of thankfully looking to Him, we say in our hearts, "My power and might has gotten me this wealth" (Deut. 8:11-17).

The Inward Look

In addition to examining the manifestations and dangers of pride, it's also important to engage in frequent and careful self-examination if we're to root out pride. That, as we've already seen, is the advice of both Jesus and Paul. The way to get the speck out of your brother's eye is, first, to get the log out of your own eye (Matt. 7:3-4). If you are a spiritual person and you want to help restore a brother or sister who has wandered astray, you must reflect upon your own walk with God (Gal. 6:1). There is no better way to spot the problem of pride in yourself than that—than through self-examination under the direction of the Spirit of God.

Even after all that, however, overcoming the spirit of pride is no easy matter. Katherine Mansfield wrote in her *Journal:*

> I wonder why it should be so difficult to be humble. I do not think that I am a good writer; I realize my faults better than anyone else could realize them. I know exactly where I fail. And yet when I have finished a story and before I have begun another, I catch myself preening my feathers. It is disheartening. There seems to be some bad old pride in my heart.[1]

Ultimately, there is only one way to effectively work at that. You need to draw even closer to God than you are. You need to confess your pride each day at the foot of the cross. You need to seek the forgiveness and strength that only God can give, and you need to assume the mind that was in Christ (Phil. 2:5). Pride is the biggest sin of all, so you're going to need the best help of all to conquer it!

---

[1]Katherine Mansfield, *Journal* (New York: Alfred A. Knopf, 1936), p. 198.

Sexual lust does not seem ugly and wrong to many persons. That is because it comes disguised as something beautiful—what is more beautiful than love? The Bible, however, has a different perspective. Jesus said that even the thought of lusting after another person is a wrong thought.

16

Overcoming Mind Pollution

Nobody is altogether free from the problem of lust. All of us have struggled with it at some time. Most people have been reluctant to admit it, but they have faced the problem nevertheless.

Jimmy Carter's admission to reporters that he, too, has struggled with sexual lust has highlighted this difficulty in a helpful way, I think. Up to that point, many would have said the idea that such feelings are wrong is antiquated and ridiculously old-fashioned. Our so-called "liberated" society had been trying to free us from such guilt-ridden notions for a long time. On the other hand, there were a lot of us who still felt, as Jimmy Carter did, that sexual lust is wrong. But we had not done very much talking about the *reality* of the struggle up until then. I wish we had, however, because the cost of not identifying sexual lust and illicit desire as something that needs to be overcome and forgiven has been a tragic one.

A lot of people laughed at Jimmy Carter's "Sunday school" confession. But Mel White asks in his new book, *The Other Side of Lust,* how laughable is the fact that during the twelve years previous to that the divorce rate doubled? How laughable is the fact that serious sex crimes involving incest, rape, and child molestation are epidemic? How laughable is the fact that venereal disease among junior high and even elementary school children is common?

Sexual lust does not seem ugly and wrong to many persons. That is because it comes disguised as something beautiful—what is more beautiful than love? The Bible, however, has a different perspective. Jesus said that even the thought of lusting after another person is a wrong thought. And in Proverbs, we read that a man who commits adultery has no sense; he is just destroying himself (Prov. 6:32-33). When you reflect on where the advocacy of unrestrained sexual freedom and gratification has been leading us, you begin to understand why.

There was a time when the word *lust* represented unbridled desire of any kind: for food, for drink, for money, for sex, for pleasure. In our time, however, we understand it mainly in terms of sexual lust. We have not said much about it, even though the sexual impulse is one of the strongest impulses we humans have. Christians have been reluctant to talk about it, and that is probably why the loud voices in favor of unlimited sexual freedom have had the hearing they've had. In the churches there has been embarrassment about addressing the subject, so the rule of silence has been observed. However, that is no longer possible, if the divorce rate, veneral disease, rape, and child molestation are going to be effectively combated.

The Exploitation of Sex

It is not sex, of course, that is wrong. It is the illicit and perverted use of it. It is the exploitation of it. It is the North American obsession with it. It is not sex that we need to speak out against. It is what man has made of it.

The exploitation of the sexual impulse is wrong, and lust is wrong, because it twists and distorts one of God's most precious gifts to us—human love. It takes out of human love its most important element—the element of covenant and commitment. It makes sex an end in itself, and gives it a priority all out of proportion with what God intended.

Sex as an end always uses people. It regards others as a means to that one consuming, self-gratifying goal. It reduces people, as almost nothing else does, to a mere animal level of behavior.

Dealing Personally With Lust

Now, back to what I started to say in the beginning. The problem is not just the problem of others. Sexual lust is not something which we deal with only on the level of putting the prostitutes and pimps and pornographers out of business. It is a problem we also have to deal with in ourselves. There is inner warfare going on in each of us. The devil is doing his best to defeat us by making self-gratification of all kinds our number one aim. Sexual lust is one of them.

Recently, when I was walking through New York's Times Square, I found myself reflecting on the problem of that warfare and how we deal with it. (When one is walking through Times Square, the thought of the problem is unavoidable.) Suddenly, it occurred to me that Times Square does not reflect the depravity of the city any more than it reflects the depravity of tourists, businessmen, and others who come there *explicitly* for the purpose of finding forbidden fruit they can't find elsewhere.

Then, I thought about myself. Away from my family, alone with problems that needed to be dealt with, worries about deadlines, and the like, it would be easy, if I allowed myself, to give in to one of the endless opportunities for sexual lust in a place like that. Then I thought about Jesus Christ, who strengthens me, who has given me the convictions I need to keep a right perspective in a situation like that. He has clearly spelled out the consequences of irresponsible behavior and compulsive self-gratification. How glad I was for that strength.

And how glad I was, too, for the knowledge of what real love is; for a wife who is strengthened and guided by Jesus Christ; for friends who share the conviction that even *thinking* immoral thoughts is something we need to confess and be ashamed of.

And how glad I was that that same Jesus Christ forgives me when I do have a momentary lapse in my thought life. He never condones such thinking, but He understands, and He forgives when it is confessed.

Impure thoughts and sexual lust can be overcome. If you will give your life to Jesus Christ, God will not only forgive you for such thoughts in the past, but He will give you strength to put them out of your mind in the present. When you come to Jesus Christ, He says, "Go and sin no more," but He does more than that—He actually helps you to sin no more.

You can determine today by God's grace that you will never commit this sin again. You can't in your own strength do that, but in Christ's strength you can, by turning your thought life over to Him right now.

Alcoholism shortens the lifespan of one out of thirteen of us by ten to twelve years; and it accounts for at least half the fatal automobile accidents. Not only that—three out of every four inmates in our prisons committed their crimes after they had been drinking!

17

Distinction Or Delusion?

One of the most incredible scandals of our day is that, out of the millions of dollars poured into research to discover preventions and cures for killer diseases, almost nothing is spent to stop the most deadly—the potentially most preventable—disease of all.

Of the major diseases in North America, significant progress is being made in fighting every one except this one. Yet, thousands of our brightest, most talented adults become its victims each year. Three of America's six Nobel Prize winners in literature—half of them— have succumbed to it. Many of the great writers of our time have been cut off by it at the height of their powers.

Not only are writers affected, but actors, politicians, doctors, teachers, factory workers, housewives—no one is safe! One out of thirteen will be stricken by it. It will cripple, incapacitate, scar families for life—and it will kill. Yet, incredible as it sounds, the governments of Canada and the United States wink at it as if it didn't exist. All the while this most deadly disease goes right on killing!

I'm talking about alcoholism, which not only shortens the lifespan of one out of thirteen of us by ten to twelve years, but also accounts for at least half the fatal accidents each year. And not only that—three of every four inmates in our prisons committed their crimes after they had been drinking!

In the United States alone, there are more than ten million problem drinkers, and drinking may be to blame for as many as 205,000 deaths a year. One-third of all suicides, half of all murders, half the automobile accidents, and a fourth of all other accidental deaths may be alcohol related, according to the federal government. Drinking may also be a prime culprit in rape, wife beating, and child abuse. Furthermore, it is associated with a number of diseases, is the third leading cause of birth defects involving retardation, and is a leading factor in juvenile crime.

Is it any wonder, then, that the Bible asks:

> Who has woe? Who has sorrow? Who has strife? Who has complaints? Who has needless bruises? Who has bloodshot eyes? Those who linger over wine, who go to sample bowls of mixed wine . . . In the end it bites like a snake and poisons like a viper (Prov. 23:29-32).

Isn't it utterly ludicrous that while governments consider bans on products with only minimal evidence of danger to human health, when it comes to this proven killer, the word is minimal? Not only does heavy drinking always result in physiological damage, but highly reliable evidence indicates that even moderate

121

drinkers incur the loss of irreplaceable brain cells every time they take a drink.[1] Your body cannot replace brain cells, you know. And every time you drink, you destroy thousands of them!

Causes of Drinking

But why do people drink? Some say for relaxation; others say for confidence, for creativity, or to forget troubles. But, as Dr. William B. Terhune, a psychiatric consultant at the Neurological Institute in New York testified: "In spite of loose talk about drinking to whet the appetite or to relax, or a little alcohol being good for the coronaries, alcohol is poor medicine—indeed useless."[2]

As for confidence, consider the fact that the kind of confidence alcohol produces causes men and women to take foolhardy chances on the road and other places, so you know that can never be a legitimate reason for taking a drink. Is alcohol a stimulant? Does it really cause you to be more creative? Does it make you more alert? No way!

On the contrary, alcohol is a depressant. Does alcohol help you forget your troubles? Usually it only creates more troubles!

So, why *do* people drink? It cannot be because it makes them better family members, clearer thinkers, or safer drivers. It cannot be because they expect any authentic benefit from drinking.

The big reason must be to gain social acceptance. Certainly that appears to be true among teen-agers. More than three million youth ages fourteen to seventeen have drinking problems in the United States. The big reason they get started seems to be the need for social approval. For teen-agers, drinking has become "an improvised rite of passage between adolescence and adulthood."[3]

Adults drink for social acceptance, too. In fact, the executive secretary of the International Commission for the Prevention of Alcoholism told an audience at the American University in Washington, D.C., a few years ago that of the six million known alcoholics in the United States that year, they would bury three-hundred-fifty-thousand before the year was out. Social pressure was the major reason for their drinking!

Social Drinking

There was a time when social drinking had a stigma attached to it. Today, the opposite is true. Not only is social drinking accepted, it is expected. You go into a restaurant, and before the waitress hands you a menu, she asks if you want a cocktail. You go to an anniversary party or to a simple get-together with friends, and the pressure to drink is on you again. Social drinking has even become fashionable in the informal gatherings of some church groups.

Frankly, I have grave doubts about the wisdom of even social drinking. The risks are simply too great. Somehow we need to strip away the glamour of social drinking.

We need to point out the physical damage that even moderate drinking can do. We need to tell the truth about the relationship between drinking and traffic deaths and injuries. We need to tell the truth about its relationship to crime, especially violent crimes. We need to tell the truth about the harm drinking does to marriages and to children.

We need to tell the truth about the necessary shallowness of relationships that depend upon a mind-dulling crutch. We need to tell the truth about the happiness that always ends with a headache.

The Indians used to call liquor "fire water." Perhaps, then, we could modify an old saying: "You can't play with fire water and not get burned." There are consequences to every decision, even the decision to indulge in only a moderate amount of drinking. What you sow you reap. And with alcohol, the harvest is always shameful and sad.

The Way Out

What do you do if you have an alcohol problem and want to get it straightened out? Let me suggest several things.

First of all, if you have an alcohol problem, you need to recognize that it is a problem.

Second, you need to recognize that alcoholism is not a problem that you or anyone else can overcome alone. You will need help.

Third, you should know that God can give you victory if you will trust Him to do so on a day-by-day basis. But you need to seek His strength for overcoming it daily!

Fourth, you should also seek the help that an organization like Alcoholics Anonymous can give you. A.A. is one of God's most useful instruments in dealing with this problem.

Finally, you need to fill your life with new purpose, by living for and in the risen Christ. Then, as the apostle Paul put it, you will be able to say from experience, "I can do everything through him who gives me strength" (Phil. 4:13).

Remember, the trend toward more and more consumption of liquor is not going to be solved ultimately by more stringent laws. It will be solved by a new attitude toward it by persons like you and me. The best way to demonstrate that attitude is to refuse to be intimidated by social pressure—in other words, to demonstrate it by example.

How about it? Don't you think it's time you had the courage to say no?

---

[1] Albert Q. Maisel, "Alcohol and Your Brain," *Reader's Digest*, June 1970, p. 68.

[2] Quoted by David Augsburger in *You Can Quit Drinking*, (Harrisonburg, Virginia: Mennonite Broadcasts, 1968), p. 3.

[3] George L. Maddox, Bevoed C. McCall in *Drinking Among Teenagers*. Quoted in "Why Teenagers Drink . . . and How Much," *U. S. News and World Report*, February 1, 1965, p. 15.

In Sannerz there must never be talk against a brother or sister, against their individual characteristics. Talking in one's own family is no exception to this, either.

18

The Law of Love

In the communal Christian community in Sannerz, which was begun in Germany in 1920, the first law was one having to do with a censorious or judgmental attitude toward others. Last November, on my birthday, some friends gave me a plaque containing that law, and it now hangs on my study wall, where it haunts me daily. Let me quote a part of it to you: "In Sannerz there must never be talk against a brother or sister, against their individual characteristics. . . . Talking in one's own family is no exception to this, either."

Jesus had some similar words to say in His Sermon on the Mount:

> Do not judge or you too will be judged. For in the same way you judge others, you will be judged, and with the measure you use, it will be measured to you. Why do you look at the speck of sawdust in your brother's eye and pay no attention to the plank in your

own eye? How can you say to your brother, "Let me take the speck out of your eye," when all the time there is a plank in your own eye? You hypocrite, first take the plank out of your own eye, and then you will see clearly to remove the speck from your brother's eye. Do not give dogs what is sacred; do not throw your pearls to pigs. If you do, they may trample them under their feet" (Matt. 7:1-6).

That statement from Jesus sends home the same point: The tendency that is in us all, to be critical and judgmental of others, is wrong. It is not the Christian way. And you and I need to hear that just as much as Jesus' disciples did or the residents of Sannerz did. None of us is in a position to cast any stones.

The picture Jesus paints is, in one sense, ridiculous. Here is this hypocrite trying to help out a poor fellow with a speck in his eye, when all the while a log is protruding from his own eye. He is so terribly concerned about another's little speck, but he cannot see the thing which is so obvious to everyone else, the mammoth problem which he, himself has!

Self-examination

But what is Jesus saying? He can't be saying that we're never to exercise any spiritual or ethical discernment, because He goes on to talk about "dogs" and "swine" and "false prophets," all of which require a certain discrimination.

Nor is He saying that there is to be no church discipline or brotherly correction, because in Matthew 18 He outlines a procedure for such admonition.

So Jesus is not saying that we should never make any

judgments at all, but, rather, that we each have a tendency to see faults in others, while overlooking those same faults in ourselves. Let me emphasize again that He is not saying that we do not make any moral judgments. He is not saying that we overlook lying and cheating and stealing and the like. That is not it at all! What He is saying is simply this: When you judge, remember that you, yourself, will be judged by the same standards you apply to others.

Every Careless Word

Now, gossip is the most obvious device with which we break this law. The chief way in which we exhibit our critical and judgmental tendencies is by talking about people. Just the other day, for example, I heard that somebody heard something about somebody, that, though probably untrue, will almost certainly ruin that person if the rumor goes much farther.

Why do we do that? Why do we perpetuate gossip and pass on rumors? If only we could remember Jesus' words to the accusers of the woman caught in adultery: "If any one of you is without sin, let him be the first to throw a stone at her" (John 8:7). If only we could remember the powerful words of the law of Sannerz: "Talking in one's own family is no exception."

Sometimes we spread gossip out of jealousy; sometimes we do so to elevate ourselves at the expense of putting someone else down; sometimes we do so out of maliciousness, even though we may not perceive it that way. But once gossip gets started, it is exceedingly difficult to nullify its effects.

James compares the tongue to the bit that turns a horse, or the rudder that turns a ship, or the spark that starts a forest fire—it is very small but very powerful.

Jesus says: "But I tell you that men will have to give account on the day of judgment for every careless word they have spoken. For by your words you will be acquitted, and by your words you will be condemned" (Matt. 12:36-37).

Numerous passages in the Bible teach the same thing, but the point is this: when we judge others, we are going to be judged too, and the measure we give is going to be the measure we get.

The way we use our tongues says a great deal about us as persons. For example, our speech may indicate whether we're trustworthy or not. It may tell whether we're kind or cruel. It may reveal our insecurity or our vanity.

However, we're going to be judged, not on the basis of our character, but on the effects our indiscretions have on others. When, because of something we've said, someone's reputation suffers, or someone loses his job, or a relationship with friends and family is hurt, then we can be sure we're going to be held accountable. The tongue can be as destructive as the sword, and there can be no excusing the indiscriminate use of it for whatever reason.

Gossip and slander are serious crimes. They do not help persons, they hurt persons. They do not reflect a loving spirit, but a venomous spirit. If only we could grasp the gravity of the crime we commit when we mis use the tongue. To malign someone can be as serious as murder.

"Go to," said the Quaker to his dog, Tray. "I will not kill thee but will merely give thee a bad name." And so he turned poor Tray into the streets with the cry of "Mad dog!" and someone else killed him.

So, the first law in Sannerz forbids censorious words

against a brother or sister. But it begins positively: "There is no law but that of love. . . . Love is joy in others. . . . Passing on the joy that the presence of others brings us means words of love."

The Other Side

Is there also a positive aspect of the words of Jesus, "For in the same way you judge others, you will be judged, and with the measure you use, it will be measured to you"? What if our judgment is not condemning, but forgiving? What if the measure we give is love instead of anger, generosity instead of jealousy—what then? What if we judge others with kind words instead of unkind words? What if we say good things about them instead of bad?

Does not the Lord's Prayer assume something about that: "Forgive us our debts as we also have forgiven our debtors"?

Perhaps you have never harmed someone outright, but have you ever hurt the character of someone by passing on a doubtful rumor, or by fabricating an untrue innuendo, or by poisoning a conversation with some unkind speculation? Perhaps you have never stolen someone's wallet, but have you ever stolen someone's personal integrity, someone's peace of mind, someone's reputation or good name?

The key to overcoming the critical spirit is self-examination. First we need to take the logs out of our own eyes.

My prayer is this, that it shall never be said of you or me that we are quick to condemn, quick to spread unfair speculation and innuendo, quick to bear a grudge. My prayer is that it may never be said of us that we are unloving and censorious in our spirit.

Examine yourself. Pray for understanding about the actions of others. Pray for a short memory as to all unkindnesses. Take sin seriously, but take forgiveness seriously, too. Remove the logs and then work at the specks—for this is the certain will of the One who taught us to judge not.

☆ ☆ ☆ ☆ ☆ ☆ ☆ ☆

TURN THE TIDE

☆ ☆ ☆ ☆ ☆ ☆ ☆ ☆

*The desire to be with others is inborn;
we see evidence of it everywhere we look.
People cling together as families. They
join organizations and clubs. They become members of cliques and gangs.
They all want to belong—to feel needed
by someone.*

19

Reach Out—Be a Friend

A young man of nineteen told me, "When I was born,
my mother put me up for adoption because I was an
accident and she didn't want me." The people who
adopted him had regarded him only as a substitute son,
he said, blaming his occasional misbehavior on a "wild
streak" inherited from his illegitimate parents. So, at
seventeen, the boy had quit school to join the Navy.

An elderly lady complained that she was unhappy
and discontented. Her husband was dead, she said, and
her children were married and had lives of their own.
"There is no place for me anymore," she confided.
"Everyone has his own interests—nobody needs me."

A recent magazine article declared, *"We are lonelier
today than our grandfathers were."* The writer of the
article spelled it out: "Crowded into smaller quarters in
big cities, surrounded by thousands of strangers, offered so much superficial entertainment, we suffer a
loneliness of restless dissatisfaction, boredom, a feeling

that we're missing something other people have."

The desire to be with others is inborn; we see evidence of it everywhere we look. People cling together as families. They join organizations and clubs. They become members of cliques and gangs. They all want to belong—to feel needed by someone.

The Peril of Loneliness

"It is not good that man should be alone." God spoke these words at the beginning of history. They are still true today.

Loneliness for many is not just a passing mood. For such, the sense of being alone and forlorn can have devastating consequences. Often they, as people, are driven to unwise and unhealthy escapes, such as alcohol and low kinds of living. They succumb to mental frustration, and many even completely withdraw from life.

Lee Harvey Oswald, charged with the murder of President Kennedy, was a child of tragedy and lovelessness. His father died before he was born. His mother was seldom at home because she had to work at a variety of jobs to support her three children. A teacher remembered that he was below average in school. "He was an introvert . . . bookish . . . a loner," she said. Clearly Oswald was an example of the principle that "it is not good that man should be alone."

Failure to Reach Out

One thing to remember, however, is that much loneliness is unnecessary. It is merely the result of thinking that friendships depend upon others' initiative rather than your own. It is due primarily to a failure to reach out, rather than a defect of character or prohibitive circumstances. So if you find that loneliness is devouring your courage and peace of mind, remember that often this feeling has no real basis. Much loneliness is not the loneliness of isolation, but the false loneliness of *insulation*, built on the pessimism of the self-centered life. As one writer put it, "Many of us are *shut-ins*, not *shut-outs*."

The writer went on to say, "We suffer a loneliness of restless dissatisfaction, boredom, a feeling that we're missing something that other people have." *Missing something that other people have*—one can't help wondering what that missing something may be.

Jesus knew the answer. His secret for overcoming loneliness is contained in His own words: "But a time is coming, and has come, when you will be scattered, each to his own home. You will leave me all alone. Yet I am not alone, for my Father is with me" (John 16:32).

What a perfect solution to the problem of loneliness—a Friend who is with you always whether you be in the crowded concrete canyons of the city or on a tiny ship in the midst of the lonely North Atlantic; whether you are the son of a poor laborer or the daughter of a millionaire executive; whether you are black or white. All you have to do is take His Word for it.

When you have the Lord for your Friend, when you have the kind of dynamic faith that must come with a friendship like that, loneliness is overcome in still another way. For such faith is impossible without participation in a community of believers.

Every live church is such a community, under the new covenant made possible by Christ. As a citizen of the covenant community, you have friendship not only on the vertical plane (with God), but also on the horizontal plane (with people). It can't be helped.

Having made the first step of faith, the rest is easy. Jesus said, "Love one another; as I have loved you."

Be a Friend

David Augsburger caught the essence of that statement when he said recently, "Friendship is not finding the right friend; it is being a friend to your friends." In relationships with persons, it is the little things that make friendships or break them. Five rules are helpful:

1. *Always take advantage of an opportunity to express pleasure over another's achievement or good fortune,* and always express sympathy in time of sorrow or trouble.
2. *Be easygoing,* the kind of person one feels comfortable with. Be easy to talk to, receptive to other people's needs and problems.
3. *Create an atmosphere of interest.* Be concerned, curious, candid, as interesting a person as you can be. Speak intelligently and stimulate others to speak.
4. *Don't be a "know-it-all."* Be humble naturally; forced humility is as obviously fake as a three-dollar bill.
5. *Equate faces with names.* Practice remembering people's names. Put real effort into the task. A person likes his name to be remembered; his name is very important to him.

Undoubtedly you will want to add a few rules of your own to this list.

In relationship with God, a dynamic, transforming faith is important. Then that faith must express itself in a supreme love for Him. If you are to love your neighbor, you must first love your God. If you are to be a friend to your neighbor, you must first be a friend to Jesus Christ.

Open your life to Him with the unconditional love He commands. You will receive in full measure His love and His friendship. And remember, God's friendship is forever.

*What do you do when you find it's im-
possible to pray? When you can't pray,
what then?*

20

When the Words Won't Come

Preachers have a wonderful penchant for gaudy prayers.
They know all the right words, and with their rhetorical
slingshots know just how to fling them heavenward. I
know! I have a whole collection of such prayers at
home. (I have even written one or two of them myself,
although most of mine didn't get far toward their
heavenly destination but ricocheted off the ceiling instead.)

If you have not had any training in the superficial art
of ecclesiastical gobbledygook, sometimes finding any
words at all seems hard. Unlike the smooth and
polished preachers you know, you have trouble finding
the right words. Sometimes it is impossible to pray.

When Tragedy Overwhelms You

Take those grief-stricken souls who have just lost a
loved one; or who have just been told they have a terminal disease; or who have just seen everything they ever

worked for all swept away in a flood. . . . How do you bring yourself to pray in circumstances like that?

Look at the psalmist's cry in Psalm 77, verses 3 and 4 (RSV):

> I think of God, and I moan;
> I meditate, and my spirit faints.
> Thou dost hold my eyelids from closing;
> I am so troubled that I cannot speak.

When You Don't Know How to Pray

But there is another reason why many find it impossible to pray. They don't know how. That is especially true of those who are just getting to know God. But it is also true for persons who have known God for a longer time. Some persons have simply never learned how to pray.

One day a pastor was visiting a long-time member of his congregation. The woman was about to undergo surgery, and the pastor suggested that the two of them pray about the operation. "You pray," said the pastor, "and then I'll close." But the woman said, "No, you'd better start the prayer too, Pastor. You see, I've never really learned how to pray." "But don't you pray the Lord's Prayer every Sunday in church?" he asked. "Yes," she said, "but I've never really learned to pray on my own. I just don't know how to go about it."

Now this may surprise you, but that pastor's experience with his long-time member was not unique. In fact, I would dare say that *most* ministers have found persons in their congregations who feel that they just don't know how to pray.

Now, obviously, they can be helped as soon as the problem is known. For one thing, all such persons have prayed without realizing it. Why? Because prayer is the

141

most natural thing in the world. Prayer is something that *all* men and women engage in—from the farmer surveying his parched ground and his withering crops to the soldier under siege. As Carlyle once wrote in a letter, "Prayer is and remains the native and deepest impulse of man." Now, when we grasp that, then, suddenly prayer does not seem as forbidding as before.

But what about those who are not yet in that position, and who, in the meantime, see *no point* in regular seasons of prayer, because they just cannot put into words the deep longings of their hearts. The task of formulating a prayer to God, even in their own secret places, is something they have never learned to do. When, *for that reason*, prayer is impossible, what then?

When You Don't Know What to Pray

But there is still another reason why persons sometimes find it difficult to pray. I've heard many prayers which include the phrase, "if it is not against Thy will." I have never felt any need to say that when I pray. I simply assume that if I pray amiss, the Lord will let me know by overruling my request. But my point is this: How do you really know you are praying according to the Lord's will? Is it possible always to know what to pray for?

Paul thought that perhaps there are times when we don't know. "We do not know what we ought to pray," he wrote to the Roman Christians (Rom. 8:26). That, to me, suggests that none of us dare claim a perfect knowledge of God's will when we pray.

Upon the contrary, so dreadfully has sin dulled our judgment, so dim is our vision of how God intricately shapes events to serve His great purposes, that we must concede that Paul was right. Certainly, there are times when we don't know how to "pray as we ought." Even with our Bibles open before us, we do not know. Even after Jesus Himself has supplied us with a pattern prayer (which we call the Lord's Prayer) we do not know. Even after having formulated thousands of private prayers of our own, we do not know. When, in our finiteness, we cannot pray because we cannot discern the will of God in a matter—what then?

When You Can't Concentrate

But Paul, in Romans 8:26, talks about still another problem that makes it impossible for us always to pray as we ought. He calls it "our weaknesses." What are some of these weaknesses?

Well, to begin with, there is the difficulty of *realizing the presence of God*. We often are aware of a sense of unreality in our praying. We wonder whether it is not just a psychological exercise we are going through. Then, there is the problem of *concentration*. We begin to pray, but suddenly we find that our minds are wandering. There is the problem of *doubt*. Is God *really* interested in my problem? we ask ourselves. And the problem of *feeling unworthy*—that is another one we need to wrestle with.

So what do you do when you find it's impossible to pray? When you can't pray (for any of the reasons I have suggested), what then?

Long ago, the Prophet Zechariah told of a time after Christ's crucifixion, when God would send the Spirit of "compassion and supplication" (Zech. 12:10, RSV). And, in Romans 8, Paul confirms that, indeed, this prophecy has come to pass. "The Spirit himself intercedes for us," Paul says (v. 26).

Thus, when it is impossible to pray—whatever the

143

reason—then the Holy Spirit is there to help us, Paul says. And what a *comfort* that is!

As Charles Spurgeon once said,

> Many a prayer that is written on the heart by the Holy Spirit seems written with faint ink, and moreover it seems to be blotted and defiled by our imperfection; but the Holy Spirit can always read His own handwriting.

So, when it's impossible to pray, why not let Him pray for you? You will never go wrong, and God will receive the Spirit's transmission of your deepest hurts and longings, your most joyous praise and most urgent petitions, without the slightest distortion.

Somewhere, I picked up this statement of William Sangster's, which sums it up beautifully: "There are times when one can pour out the heart to God in a torrent of words, but never let it be thought that prayer is for the fluent only. Even the most inarticulate can pray. When grief, or disappointment, or sin strikes one dumb, there is still the upward look."

The greatest men and women are not always the most gifted! Often God comes into the life of a man or a woman of very ordinary ability and uses that person mightily.

21

Entrusted With Talents

Jesus told a story about three men who were each entrusted with a certain amount of money while their master was away. They were given the money according to their abilities. The first man got $5,000. The second man got $2,000. And the third man got $1,000.

True to form, the man with first-rate abilities doubled his $5,000. So did the man with second-rate abilities. But the third-rate man said to himself, "Why invest the money and take a chance on losing it all?" So he simply hid his $1,000—he buried it safely. Perhaps he thought to himself that the banks might fail, or maybe the man just did not trust banks. Whatever the reason, he played it safe.

We could react in a number of ways. We might say, "Well, isn't that exactly what we should have expected? Third-rate people give third-rate performances, that's all. The master should have known better than to even give him the thousand!" Or if we, ourselves, feel we fit into the category of "average" or "below average," we might tend to be more sympathetic and say, "Well, those are the breaks. The first two guys got lucky. The third guy was careful, thought he'd better not be a gambler and take any chances—and he gets the black eye!" Or you could respond that the master had no right to be so hard on him. You could argue that at least this poor fellow's simple approach to life had something in it that was more noble than the master's materialism.

Come to think of it, that would be a pretty good argument. We have placed a premium on getting ahead in our society, haven't we? With Emerson, we have shouted, "Hitch your wagon to a star, young man!" With Troy Moore, we've said, "Aim high! It's no harder on your gun to shoot the feathers off an eagle than the fur off a skunk!" But, in reality, ambition is a bull elephant gone mad, blindly trampling over everything that's in its way! Ambition becomes an end in itself—a dead end!

But that could not have been the point of Jesus' story, because it is the man of marginal ability, the man without any ambition, who gets rebuked.

Overwhelmed by Bigness

Or could it have been the point? Listen to this statement, for example. (It is part of his explanation to his master as to why he simply buried the money.) "Master, I knew that you are a hard man, harvesting where you have not sown and gathering where you have not scattered seed. So I was afraid" (Matt. 25:24-25). His statement betrays the fact that he was overwhelmed by bigness. He was absolutely awed by his master's abilities. What a man his master was! There was no telling what he might do with $1,000—probably triple it in a week! "But with my luck," he could have said to

146

himself, "I'd lose it on my way to the bank." So, instead of investing the money, he buried it.

That's why the master rebuked him! He knew the man's limitations, yet he was willing to trust him with a portion of his wealth. He was willing to give him a chance at least to use what ability he had. He was willing to risk $1,000 to help him see that those who are less endowed can play roles every bit as important as the gifted.

Yet, instead of being grateful for the chance, what did the man do? He retreated into the protective shell of his inferiority complex. He could have handled the $1,000, but he allowed himself to be defeated by his fear of defeat. The sole reason for his failure was that he was so awed by success that he was afraid to fail. Probably he said something like this to himself: "What can I do? What's the use of me competing with those who easily leave me far behind? What's the use of trying to collect my little interest on the thousand when somebody else knows how to double it? No, there are others better suited for the job—let them do it."

Everybody Counts

What a tragedy such an attitude is. First of all, it fails altogether to recognize that the work of the world, the majority of it, the brunt of it, is shouldered by men and women of modest ability. We need the geniuses, but we need the men and women of common ability, too. The architect may design his skyscraper, but without the brick layer and the plumber and the electrician it will never come to life.

The princes of the pulpit may preach their sermons and the theologians may write their monographs, but without the faithful Sunday school teachers, without the deacons, without the saints who flesh out their Christianity seven days a week, without the parents who are concerned about their children's spiritual welfare, the church would go nowhere.

Duets, Not Solos

In the second place, let us also remember that the greatest performances are seldom solos. Think of what Edison owed to his assistants. Think of what Lincoln owed to his mother. Think of those who have prepared you for your greatest achievements, and who assisted you in them. And think of those whose work had gone before. No, greatness is not a solo effort. Greatness always stands upon the shoulders of common, ordinary persons like you and me.

Greatness Depends on God, Not Gifts

Finally, let us remember that the greatest men and women are not always the most gifted! Often, God comes into the life of a man or a woman of very ordinary ability and uses that person mightily. Think of Moses, or Peter, or Paul before God came along.

Don't you bury that chance when it comes! Don't you dare! Don't take a chance on failing God and failing the rest of us, just because you're afraid of personal failure and embarrassment. God has the peculiar habit of bypassing the great and the powerful of this world and putting His hand on the shoulder of people like you . . . like me! Don't go running for cover when He comes to you. Use your talents, whatever they may be! Use your opportunities, whenever they may come!

God expects us to use the gifts He has entrusted to us, no matter how few or how many. He is not really a hard taskmaster as the one-talent man imagined. He asks only that we use the abilities and opportunities He has entrusted to us for His glory and for the edification and the ministry of the church. But to bury them because of a false feeling of inferiority is just as irresponsible as to squander them—in the end it is the same.

In the story, the spotlight is on the man of third-rate ability. But it could just as easily have been on either of the other two had they, for whatever reason, squandered their gifts. No matter which category you fall into, the spotlight could be on you.

We are all responsible for the gifts we've been endowed with. How we use them is of eternal significance. Never forget, it's not what you have, but how you use what you have, that determines in God's book whether you are third-rate or first!

We are living in a world that promises wholeness but tears you apart, that promises peace of mind but, instead, produces restlessness.

22

Blessed Is the One-Track Mind

When I was a boy, a carnival came to town almost every summer. And they were not like the little fairs that we have today to raise money for the local fire department or rescue squad. They were real carnivals! They had glamour and glitter, sounds and smells, delirious colors, delicious confections, and a delightful confusion that couldn't be matched by any other experience on record in my boyish mind.

In retrospect, it is difficult for me to understand why I had such keen interest in carnivals. I got sick on the food. I got sick on the rides. And I think there were even a few times when I got sick just because I was so keyed up by the big event. There is only one way I can understand my excitement at carnival times. I must understand it in terms of the glamour and the glitter and the delightful confusion of the event. Fortunately, I've long since outgrown carnival fever, but when you're a boy it's easy to let your mind be teased by the spectacle of such a happening. When you're a boy the fantastic world of carnival time seems, for the moment at least, to be what life's all about.

When Life Is a Carnival

But what is life all about for mature men and women? What is life all about for twentieth-century adults? When I read my newspaper and magazines, I am convinced that what it's all about for a great many people is nothing more than a kind of grown-ups' carnival time. The good word seems to be that at last we are beyond the days of dark superstition, drear puritanism, and drab provincialism—at least in California and Nevada, and in the big cities and a few other such places. Finally, we're told, we've graduated from all that, and success, sex, and freedom from moral restrictions are the things that life's all about. What life is all about, we're told, is getting free from the confining morality of the past and allowing our adultish minds to be tickled by the glamour and the glitter, the sounds and the smells, and the delirious, delicious, delightful collage of carnival time U.S.A. However, the trouble is that we get sick, as in the carnival times of our youth. That is not really a happy time at all. And in the places where supposedly the ideal of our age has become reality, despair and suicide are epidemic.

We are living in a world that promises wholeness but tears you apart, that promises peace of mind but, instead, produces restlessness. Men and women looking for a set of values to live by are confronted with all manner of possibilities which, selected indiscriminately, leave the mind in disarray like rummage sale tables, or like an attic in which all sorts of things have been stored away without any order whatsoever.

I was thinking about these things one night not long ago when I was watching John Ruth's film on the Amish on Public TV. Many things would prevent me from becoming an Amishman, but when I watched the film, I knew something was there—something solid, something substantial, something stable, something secure, something that is missing in the carnival time scene, something that is only found where God—not glitter —is in focus.

Distractions

Let me test this with you. I think the reason for the difference boils down to this. The carnival time scene is basically a distraction. There are all sorts of bright, flashing lights and shiny, shimmering trifles demanding a piece of our attention. But God is not a distraction. Just because of who He is, He demands *all* of our attention. He seeks not a piece of our mind, but all of it!

Do you remember the story in the Bible about Jesus visiting the home of Mary and Martha? Martha was busy in the kitchen getting everything tidied up and the food prepared, while Mary was in the living room sitting at the feet of Jesus. Mary was listening to His teaching, and we read,

> But Martha was distracted by all the preparations that had to be made. She came to him and asked, "Lord, don't you care that my sister has left me to do the work by myself? Tell her to help me!"
>
> "Martha, Martha," the Lord answered, "You are worried and upset about many things, but only one thing is needed. Mary has chosen what is better, and it will not be taken away from her!" (Luke 10:40-42).

Double-Mindedness

It is no coincidence that the Bible speaks of the man who is caught up in distractions as a double-minded man. James uses the word twice. The first time is in chapter 1, verse 8, where he describes the double-minded man as "unstable in all he does." The second time is in chapter 4, verse 8, where he says that the double-minded man needs to purify his heart, which in biblical language means he needs to get his mind on a single track.

The meaning of the word "double-minded" is not difficult. James is simply talking of the man who has doubts about God because he is distracted by the glamour and glitter of the world's lusts and temptations. Do you remember Mr. Facing-Both-Ways in John Bunyan's *Pilgrim's Progress?* Do you remember the prophets of Baal on Mt. Carmel? Because of them, Elijah had to ask the people, "How long are you going to halt between two opinions?" Do you remember how Augustine prayed one time, "O Lord, grant me purity, but not yet"?

In the first chapter of James' epistle, he says that the double-minded man is a man who is like a wave of the sea that is tossed and driven by the wind. That is an apt description of men and women today. A restlessness, an inner tempest, is raging that makes a great many people miserable and unhappy. The need to always get out and do something is one manifestation of it—the need for the stimulus of pleasure, of alcohol, of drugs.

People no longer have peace of mind. They no longer know how to sit down and enjoy a good book or enjoy their families or pray.

They think that happiness and peace of mind is

something that you attain, but it is not. It is, rather, a by-product. When you go after peace of mind as an end in itself, you will always miss it. Instead, it is a by-product of getting rid of the distractions, by focusing your mind and heart on one thing basically. As Jesus put it long ago, "But seek first his kingdom and his righteousness, and all these things [including peace of mind and happiness] will be given to you as well" (Matt. 6:33).

That is what James means when he says that we are to purify our hearts. The pure heart is the heart that is no longer divided or distracted. James is asking of us an undivided love toward God, a love which regards God as our highest good and keeps its focus on Him.

It is God, of course, who brings about the transformation in our lives that gives us peace of mind. But that does not mean that we remain passive in the matter. James says (in 4:8), "Come near to God and He will come near to you."

So, today, why don't *you* turn from the distractions, from the glitter and the glamour that keep you from getting close to God, and set your mind on Him and Him alone? Experience for yourself the blessedness of the one-track mind.

Stress comes to all men and women in all generations. The question, then, is not whether you must face stress, but what you will do with it.

23

Living Without Strain

This is the age
Of the half-read page,
And the quick hash
And the mad dash.
The bright night
With the nerves tight.
The plane hop
With the brief stop.
The lamp tan
In a short span.
The Big Shot
In a good spot.
And the brain strain
And the heart pain.
And the cat naps
Till the spring snaps—
And the fun's done![1]

Something about that little poem really catches the essence of these days, doesn't it? It was written over thirty years ago, but, if anything, we are in more of a hurry now than we were then—and more caught up with creature comforts and getting to the top, too.

No wonder, then, that stress has become one of the most dangerous enemies of physical and emotional well-being. It affects persons in every age group: children, young adults, middle-aged persons, and even the elderly.

Children in our day, for example, often find themselves in the middle when their parents' marriages are on the rocks. Newlyweds find themselves in the unenviable position of having to make the traditional adjustments with respect to the handling of finances, the choosing of social and recreational activities, and the blending of moral and spiritual values. They also have other adjustments forced on them by a society whose whole orientation is concerned with productivity and getting ahead.

And the elderly, because of stress factors like illness, widowhood, retirement, receiving welfare, and living alone, are also caught, often resulting in the social withdrawal known as disengagement.

However, that is not really the whole picture. Stress has been the lot of other generations too, though we are prone to forget it. Think, for example, of the fate of many a child before the day of child labor laws. Or think of the stress that came upon young families in the two terrible World Wars of this century, and of those in other wars. Auden describes our times as "the age of anxiety," but how does that differ from Paine's description of 1776, in which he declared, "These are times that try men's souls"?

Even Jesus needed to contend with stress, you will remember. First, there was the pressure of a deadline: "As long as it is day, we must do the work of him who sent me. Night is coming, when no one can work" (John 9:4). Then there was the strain of an impossible decision: "Father, if it is possible, may this cup be taken from me. Yet not as I will, but as you will" (Matt. 26:39). Then there was the inner distress of spirit, because of the difficulties He faced: "Now my heart is troubled" (John 12:27). So, even Jesus needed to grapple with the difficulty of stress.

Mark tells about a time when, even though Jesus arose before daybreak to be alone for meditation and prayer, Peter and the disciples burst into His quiet time with, "Where have you been? Everybody's looking for you!"

Luke tells us about a difficult face-to-face confrontation between Jesus and the devil shortly after Jesus' baptism. John tells us how Jesus' brothers tried to pressure Him into going into Jerusalem prematurely.

Matthew tells how the Palm Sunday crowds attempted to force Jesus into the role of a military Messiah. The author of Hebrews tells us that He had to face the very same trials and temptations that we have to face, and we know that, later on, the apostles did, too.

Thus, while we do live in rather maddening times, and while we are under constant and tremendous pressures, nevertheless our lot is not really so different from past generations. Stress, though they may not have identified it as we have, was their dilemma, too. They had a fair share of pressures with which to contend. Stress, like trouble, comes to all men and women in all generations.

The question, then, is not *whether* you must face

stress, but what you will do with it, how you will respond to it.

In his book, *Turning Your Stress Into Strength,* Robert Schuller tells about two boys who were raised by an alcoholic father. When they finally were old enough to leave home, each boy went his separate way. Years later, a psychologist, who was making a study of the effect of alcoholic parents on children, studied the report one of his assistants made of interviews with the two men. One was a sharp, successful individual who never took a drink. The other was a hopeless, helpless drunk like his father. The researcher had asked each one individually why he turned out as he had. The answer they gave was identical: "What else could you expect when you had a father like mine?"

That story serves to illustrate that it's not the stress that makes the difference, but how you respond to it. Suppose, for example, that you have just received a crushing blow. A position you have been working toward for many years and which you thought would be yours has been given to someone else, a relative newcomer to the scene. You might respond by saying, "O.K., I'm disappointed but, now, what I have to decide is, where do I go from here?" On the other hand, you might become so upset you lose control completely and have an anxiety reaction necessitating a brief hospital stay. Or you might withdraw and become immersed for years in a tearful pool of self-pity and resentment.

Let me get right to the point of discussing how to avoid one of the latter responses in such situations.

First, determine how wrapped up you are in yourself. If *you* are all-important and you have never really learned what it means to love your neighbor as yourself,

158

you will make responses similar to one of the latter two in every situation, and the result will be inner turmoil. But if you can learn instead to live the following prescriptions of Jesus, you will possess some of the most important resources of all for moving from stress to serenity. Here they are:

Prescription #1: "Do not think of yourself more highly than you ought, but rather think of yourself with sober judgment" (Rom. 12:3).

Prescription #2: "Love your neighbor as yourself" (Luke 10:27).

Prescription #3: "Do nothing out of selfish ambition or vain conceit, but in humility consider others better than yourselves. Each of you should look not only to your own interests, but also to the interests of others" (Phil. 2:3-4).

Second, ask yourself how much faith you have that God will see you through stressful circumstances. Do you really believe what the Bible says about God's not allowing any trial to come which you cannot bear? If so, try these prescriptions—believe them and live them:

Prescription #1: "Come to me, all you who are weary and burdened, and I will give you rest" (Matt. 11:28).

Prescription #2: "Be still, and know that I am God" (Ps. 46:10, KJV).

Believe me, if you employ these two principles, you will be able to travel light. If you will be as interested in the well-being of others as you are in your own, and if you will put quiet confidence in God, you will have come far in your ability to make the right choices and to move from stress to serenity and strength.

[1]Virginia Brasier, reprinted from *The Saturday Evening Post* (Philadelphia: Curtis Publishing Company, May 28, 1949), p. 72. Copyright 1949 The Curtis Publishing Company.

There are those who suggest that Christians usually come to God in a moment of weakness. It may be under the threat of hell, in the grip of a terminal disease, or at the threshold of an emotional breakdown. But usually it is in weakness that men and women embrace the Christian faith.

24

Is Faith a Crutch?

The accusation that religion is a crutch takes many curtain calls in a day when self-sufficiency is lauded. Our day is such a day, and we are all familiar with the charge. Some of us have encountered it in atheistic writers like Theodore Dreiser, who defined religion as "a bandage that man has invented to protect a soul made bloody by circumstance." Others of us have heard the definition given by Ambrose Bierce, that religion is "a daughter of Hope and Fear, explaining to Ignorance the nature of the Unknowable." But we have all heard it said somewhere that religion is for the weak and faint of heart. With William Ernest Henley, modern man declares: "I am master of my fate; I am the captain of my soul." And to say otherwise is to prove you've never learned to stand on your own two feet, and that you are caught in the vice-grip of superstition.

In the courtroom of our minds, this indictment is not lightly dismissed. Each of us needs to wrestle with it and come to a verdict. Each of us needs to weigh the evidence. Each of us needs to hear the arguments, and some of them are powerful.

For example, in support of the contention that religion is a daughter of Fear, it is pointed out that Christians usually come to God in a moment of weakness. It may be under the threat of hell. It may be in the grip of a terminal disease. It may be at the threshold of an emotional breakdown. It may be in the winter of life when death suddenly takes on cold reality. But it is usually in weakness that men and women embrace religion, we are told.

And in support of the contention that religion is a crutch for those who never learned to think for themselves, it is argued that the church is a follower of society. The church is not a leader; it has no vision; it is the champion of the status quo; and it lacks the breadth of perception contained in the scientific world view.

A Powerful Appeal

These are persuasive arguments that have a ring of truth. Their appeal is powerful, and they are not easily ignored. As a matter of fact, when we try to ignore them, we appear to affirm them. When we dismiss outright the accusation that religion is a crutch, we appear to demonstrate that we really cannot stand on our own two feet. Because we tenaciously cling to that for which we will not fight, we appear to have proven that Christianity is no more than a placebo, a security blanket, a crutch for the weak and those whose vision is restricted.

So, we cannot run from the charge. We must have our day in court. Otherwise, we will be like that Arab who decided to have a midnight snack of dates. In the candlelight in his tent he picked up a date, happened to notice there was a worm in it, and threw it aside. Upon examination of a second date, he discovered that it, too, had a worm in it, so he threw it aside. Then he blew out the candle and proceeded to eat the rest of his bowl of dates.

Now surely we do not want to approach our religion as the Arab approached his bowl of dates. There are some, of course, who do that. We all know some persons who approach religion as a drug. Karl Marx was not entirely wrong when he said that religion is the opiate of the people, because for some people it is! Religion is every bit as much of an escape to them as alcohol is for others. Without a doubt, in every congregation there are a few for whom Christianity is merely a pleasant pill, a source of comfort in an uncomfortable world. When their Christianity is threatened, instead of facing the challenge, they retreat even further into their fantasy land. You see, to them comfort is more important than truth.

True Christians, however, have no such reluctance to face the issues, and that includes the accusation that religion is a crutch, a wishful dream. True Christians are not escapists. True Christians are not dreamers. They are supreme realists! And it, therefore, behooves the critics of Christianity to be absolutely certain that they do not judge the whole by the few.

After all, we would not think of judging art by a few impoverished comic strips. We would not think of judging music by the hard rock detonations that blast from the stereos of teen-agers. We would not think of judging literature by the pornographic periodicals that are peddled at newsstands, or by sensationalistic tabloids. Nor should we judge Christianity by the fairyland mirage that has been embraced by a misguided few.

No doubt the mirage is a crutch for those who lack

inner fortitude and inner vision, but genuine Christianity is just the opposite. It is not a bomb shelter. It is not a comfortable hiding place in which those who are afraid of life may retreat. Upon the contrary, there is no way of life that requires more vulnerability, more invincibility, or more durability than the Christian way of life. True religion, true Christianity, is always difficult precisely because it is not a retreat, but an enlistment of supreme allegiance. Jesus made that incontrovertibly clear: "And anyone who does not carry his cross and follow me cannot be my disciple" (Luke 14:27). And again, "In the same way, any of you who does not give up everything he has cannot be my disciple" (Luke 14:33). Does that sound like a crutch? Does that sound like retreat? Does that sound like an escapist's refuge?

Empty Rhetoric?

There are some who would dismiss these statements of Jesus as empty rhetoric, but Jesus' life and death was not empty rhetoric. Nor have the lives of saints who have borne out His words been empty rhetoric.

Hear the words of Peter, for example: "We have left everything to follow you!" (Matt. 19:27). Does that sound like empty rhetoric?

Hear the words of Paul: "Five times I received from the Jews the forty lashes minus one. Three times I was beaten with rods, once I was stoned, three times I was shipwrecked, I spent a night and a day in the open sea, I have been constantly on the move. I have been in danger from rivers, in danger from bandits, in danger from my own countrymen, in danger from Gentiles; in danger in the city, in danger in the country, in danger at sea; and in danger from false brothers. I have labored and toiled and have often gone without sleep; I have known hunger and thirst and have often gone without food; I have been cold and naked. Besides everything else, I face daily the pressure of my concern for all the churches" (2 Cor. 11:24-28). Does that sound like empty rhetoric?

The author of Hebrews, surveying the role of Old Testament saints, begins to illustrate this very fact. But after a long chapter he finally has to admit, "I do not have time to tell about Gideon, Barak, Samson, Jephthah, David, Samuel and the prophets, who through faith conquered kingdoms, administered justice, and gained what was promised; who shut the mouths of lions, quenched the fury of the flames, and escaped the edge of the sword; whose weakness was turned to strength; and who became powerful in battle and routed foreign armies. . . Others were tortured and refused to be released . . . Some faced jeers and flogging, while still others were chained and put in prison. They were stoned; they were sawed in two; they were put to death by the sword. They went about in sheepskins and goatskins, destitute, persecuted and mistreated . . . They wandered in deserts and mountains, and in caves and holes in the ground" (Heb. 11:32-38). Were their lives empty rhetoric?

But do not stop there! Think about the saints of Reformation times who stood for the faith in spite of fire, dungeon, and sword. Think about the martyrs of our own times, the John and Betty Stams, the Jim Elliots, and the Paul Carlsons. The history of the church is a recital of strength and steadfastness in the face of the most difficult circumstances imaginable.

But what of the argument that the decision to become a Christian is an emotional one made in weakness? That is an objection heard frequently, to which we may respond: Is the decision to reject God less emotionally motivated? Take a man like Theodore Dreiser. What caused him to turn against religion and God? Was it a purely intellectual conviction of the tenets of socialism? Or were both his rejection of God and of capitalism the result of his bitter emotional reaction to a social system and a religious naivete which he thought had shackled his immigrant parents and their fifteen children in irons of perpetual poverty? Undoubtedly it was the latter.

His decision to reject God was not primarily intellectual, but the result of a gnawing frustration with life. Of course, every decision has its intellectual aspects too, but to object to Christian faith because it is partly motivated by emotion is to open a whole bag of parallel conclusions that religion's accusers would not accept in ten thousand years!

Furthermore, since when is the recognition of need weakness? It takes courage to admit need. It may be that a man or woman will have to come to the end of him or herself to finally acknowledge it; nevertheless, even then it takes guts to relinquish pride and step out in faith. They are not weak, then, who turn to Christ, but humbled and conscious of a need. On the other hand, I am convinced that there are many who, having come to the end of themselves, accept that state as their lifelong fate. They give up rather than admit their need. From there on, they simply exist. That, it seems to me, is the weak position. They think that it is courage, but the truth is that it is the weakness of stubborn pride.

A Resource, Not a Refuge

Is Christianity, then, a blind escape? Is it that sort of refuge? No, it is rather a resource! It is a source of strength, a source of purpose, a source of life, and a source of hope that knows no parallel. From whence came the emotional and physical strength of the great heroes of the faith? Where did they get their courage? They got it from God!

From whence comes faith's affirmation that there is more to this universe than what can be detected by man's five senses and by means of technological aids? God has given this revelation through the Bible, the written Word; and through Christ, the living Word! It is not the religious man whose vision is restricted; it is the self-sufficient man of the world!

Do not be deceived, then, by the restricted vision of those whose universe is a closed system. It is not the Christless man who is the crutchless man. On the contrary, the man whose God is the security of self-sufficiency is the least secure of all, for he has confined himself to himself. Since he lives for no one else, he can depend upon no one else. He becomes his own crutch. His only resource is his bankrupt self. He is an island surrounded on the north, east, south, and west by himself. And beyond himself there is no meaning.

The great trial lawyer, Clarence Darrow, who was such a man, hopelessly affirmed, "The outstanding fact that cannot be dodged by thoughtful men is the futility of it all." And Bertrand Russell admitted, "Only on the firm foundation of unyielding despair, can the soul's habitation be safely built." That is the alternative of atheism! "The futility of it all!" "Unyielding despair!"

No wonder, then, that men turn inward to themselves; they have nowhere else to turn! But that is not strength; that is retreat. Inevitably it leads to some form of self-gratification as one's chief end in life, which in the face of meaninglessness is retreat, a temporary drug, an escape from despair that leads back to despair on that fateful day when the great Creator and Judge says, "You fool! This very night your life will be demanded from you. Then who will get what you have prepared for yourself?" (Luke 12:20).

Christians, however, look beyond self, not to a celestial Never-Never Land, but to a reality and to a Person—not to one who keeps them from trouble, but One who sees them through it—whose grace is sufficient and who enables them to do all things. No, the Christian faith is not a crutch; it is the victory that overcomes the world!

25

The Last Word

Few of us go through life without a considerable load of dead weight on our shoulders. Sometimes it is the result of crises or troubles that come into our lives; sometimes it is the weight of patterns we cannot alter (and there is nothing heavier than that—a habit you can't overcome). Other times the weight is caused by an inner tide of negativism—"Who would ever want *my* friendship?" "I just don't have what it takes." "I can't pray—what's the use of trying?" But we don't need to be bent over by burdens. We can decide at any moment, "From now on, I'm traveling light!"

I've spent quite a few pages describing the nature of some of the burdens we bear. I've suggested a few insights I hope will be helpful. In the section headings I've shared four simple principles which have helped me significantly: transfer the load of your burdens to God; transform the past and future by letting Him guide you today; trade in old habits for new ones God wants to teach you; and turn the tide of negativism by becoming more wrapped up in Him and less wrapped up in you.

I trust I've been faithful in the things I've shared, but I thought the last word ought to be His. Here, then, are some appropriate thoughts He wants to share. I leave the application to His Spirit and you.

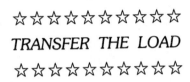

TRANSFER THE LOAD

Transfer the load of your burdens to God.

Burdens

"Come to me, all you who are weary and burdened, and I will give you rest. Take my yoke upon you and learn from me, for I am gentle and humble in heart, and you will find rest for your souls. For my yoke is easy and my burden is light" (Matt. 11:28-30).

Crises

"A righteous man may have many troubles, but the Lord delivers him from them all." (Ps. 34:19).

Troubles

"For our light and momentary troubles are achieving for us an eternal glory that far outweighs them all" (2 Cor. 4:17).

☆ ☆ ☆ ☆ ☆ ☆ ☆ ☆ ☆ ☆ ☆ ☆

TRANSFORM
THE PAST AND FUTURE

☆ ☆ ☆ ☆ ☆ ☆ ☆ ☆ ☆ ☆ ☆

Transform the past and the future by letting Him guide you today.

Regrets

"Forget the former things; do not dwell on the past. See, I am doing a new thing! Now it springs up; do you not perceive it? I am making a way in the desert and streams in the wasteland" (Isa. 43:18-19).

Guilt

"If we confess our sins, he is faithful and just and will forgive us our sins and purify us from all unrighteousness" (1 John 1:9).

Failure

"Not that I have already obtained all this, or have already been made perfect, but I press on to take hold of that for which Christ Jesus took hold of me. Brothers, I do not consider myself yet to have taken hold of it. But one thing I do: Forgetting what is behind and straining toward what is ahead, I press on toward the goal to win the prize for which God has called me heavenward in Christ Jesus" (Phil. 3:12-14).

Aging

"They will still bear fruit in old age, they will stay fresh and green, proclaiming, 'The Lord is upright; he is my Rock, and there is no wickedness in him'" (Ps. 92:14-15).

Death

"I tell you the truth, if a man keeps my word, he will never see death" (John 8:51).

Worry

"Therefore I tell you, do not worry about your life, what you will eat or drink; or about your body, what you will wear. Is not life more important than food, and the body more important than clothes? Look at the birds of the air; they do not sow or reap or store away in barns, and yet your heavenly Father feeds them. Are you not much more valuable than they? Who of you by worrying can add a single hour to his life?

"And why do you worry about clothes? See how the lilies of the field grow. They do not labor or spin. Yet I tell you that not even Solomon in all his splendor was dressed like one of these. If that is how God clothes the grass of the field, which is here today and tomorrow is thrown into the fire, will he not much more clothe you, O you of little faith? So do not worry, saying, 'What shall we eat?' or 'What shall we drink?' or 'What shall we wear?' For the pagans run after all these things, and your heavenly Father knows that you need them. But seek first his kingdom and his righteousness, and all these things will be given to you as well. Therefore do not worry about tomorrow, for tomorrow will worry about itself. Each day has enough trouble of its own" (Matt. 6:25-34).

☆ ☆ ☆ ☆ ☆ ☆ ☆ ☆ ☆ ☆

TRADE IN OLD HABITS

☆ ☆ ☆ ☆ ☆ ☆ ☆ ☆ ☆ ☆

Trade in your old habits for new ones that God wants to teach you.

Gluttony

"You eat, but never have enough. You drink, but never have your fill . . . This is what the Lord Almighty says: 'Give careful thought to your ways'" (Hag. 1:6-7).

Laziness

"We do not want you to become lazy, but to imitate those who through faith and patience inherit what has been promised" (Heb. 6:12).

Avarice

"The brother in humble circumstances ought to take pride in his high position. But the one who is rich should take pride in his low position, because he will pass away like a wild flower. For the sun rises with scorching heat and withers the plant; its blossom falls and its beauty is destroyed. In the same way, the rich man will fade away even while he goes about his business" (James 1:9-11).

Jealousy

"If you harbor bitter envy and selfish ambition in your hearts, do not boast about it or deny the truth. Such 'wisdom' does not come down from heaven but is earthly, unspiritual, of the devil. For where you have envy and selfish ambition, there you find disorder and every evil practice " (James 3:14-16).

Anger

"In your anger do not sin; when you are on your beds, search your hearts and be silent" (Ps. 4:4).

Pride

"For by the grace given me I say to every one of you: Do not think of yourself more highly than you ought, but rather think of yourself with sober judgment, in accordance with the measure of faith God has given you. Just as each of us has one body with many members, and these members do not all have the same function, so in Christ we who are many form one body, and each member belongs to all the others. We have different gifts, according to the grace given us. If a man's gift is prophesying, let him use it in proportion to his faith. If it is serving, let him serve; if it is teaching, let him teach; if it is encouraging, let him encourage; if it is contributing to the needs of others, let him give generously; if it is leadership, let him govern diligently; if it is showing mercy, let him do it cheerfully" (Rom. 12:3-8).

Lust

"My son, keep your father's commands and do not forsake your mother's teaching. Bind them upon your heart forever; fasten them around your neck. When you walk, they will guide you; when you sleep, they will watch over you; when you awake, they will speak to you. For these commands are a lamp, this teaching is a light, and the corrections of discipline are the way to life, keeping you from the immoral woman, from the smooth tongue of the wayward wife. Do not lust in your heart after her beauty or let her captivate you with her eyes, for the prostitute reduces you to a loaf of bread, and the adulteress preys upon your very life" (Prov. 6:20-26).

Alcoholism

"Do not get drunk on wine, which leads to debauchery. Instead, be filled with the Spirit" (Eph. 5:18).

Gossip

"Brothers, if someone is caught in a sin, you who are spiritual should restore him gently. But watch yourself, or you also may be tempted. Carry each other's burdens, and in this way you will fulfill the law of Christ. If anyone thinks he is something when he is nothing, he deceives himself" (Gal. 6:1-3).

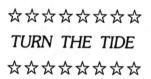

TURN THE TIDE

Turn the tide of negativism by becoming more wrapped up in Him and less wrapped up in you.

Loneliness

"We proclaim to you what we have seen and heard, so that you also may have fellowship with us. And our fellowship is with the Father and with his Son, Jesus Christ. We write this to make our joy complete" (1 John 1:3-4).

Prayerlessness

"In the same way, the Spirit helps us in our weakness.

We do not know what we ought to pray, but the Spirit himself intercedes for us with groans that words cannot express. And he who searches our hearts knows the mind of the Spirit, because the Spirit intercedes for the saints in accordance with God's will" (Rom. 8:26-27).

Inferiority Complex

"So then, men ought to regard us as servants of Christ and as those entrusted with the secret things of God. Now it is required that those who have been given a trust must prove faithful" (1 Cor. 4:1-2).

Restlessness

"Be patient, then, brothers, until the Lord's coming. See how the farmer waits for the land to yield its valuable crop and how patient he is for the fall and spring rains. You, too, be patient and stand firm, because the Lord's coming is near" (James 5:7-8).

Stress

"Blessed is the man who perseveres under trial, because when he has stood the test, he will receive the crown of life that God has promised to those who love him" (James 1:12).

Doubts

"See to it, brothers, that none of you has a sinful, unbelieving heart that turns away from the living God. But encourage one another daily, as long as it is called Today, so that none of you may be hardened by sin's deceitfulness. We have come to share in Christ if we hold firmly till the end the confidence we had at first" (Heb. 3:12-14).